Futures
Open to Variety

A manual for the wise use of the later-than-now

Stefan Bergheim

ISBN: 978-3-00-069053-2

Publisher:

ZGF Publishers
Dr. Stefan Bergheim
Wilhelm-Busch-Str. 45
60431 Frankfurt am Main
Germany

stefan.bergheim@zukuenfte.net

Cover and illustration: Heike Jane Zimmermann

Print and distribution: IngramSpark

For Carla and Felix

Contents

Preface to the English Edition

The original German edition of this book was written with two intentions in mind. First and foremost, to bring the insights and methods of the global Futures Literacy network to German-speaking countries. Among those insights is the use of futures in the plural, which is still highly unusual in German: Using "Zukünfte" rather than just "Zukunft" still meets a lot of resistance. Second, to share my experience with practical futures-oriented processes that I have led or advised over the past decade.

After publishing the German edition of the book in late 2020, two sets of demands were expressed by the international network: The first was the demand for a comprehensive publication in English that builds on the ideas of Futures Literacy and that is easy to understand. The second was an interest within the futures field in the topic of wellbeing, quality of life, or progress. This is the area that I have been working in for the past 15 years. Most of the case studies in the third part of the book relate to it.

Both the English and the German editions are meant to be manuals for the wise use of the later-than-now. They both aim to inspire the readers to start or to improve futures-related processes. They are an introduction to a set of futures methods that I found particularly helpful. And they provide practical insights from processes that I facilitated or advised.

If you happen to be a futurist with many years of practice and a deep understanding of methods and theories, you might still be interested in the introductory chapters on dialogue, powerful questions, and German systems theory. You also might appreciate chapters 17 to 19 that deal with wellbeing processes in Germany. And you may not yet be familiar with the methods of Future Search and Appreciative Inquiry as presented in chapters 10 and 13.

Given the original intention and my own geographic and cultural base, the book is biased towards examples and experiences from Germany. But I hope the readers can easily link these to their own experiences in their contexts – either by highlighting similarities or differences.

This English edition was supported by the translation software deepl.com and by April K. Ward. Of course, full responsibility for the final text lies with me.

Stefan Bergheim

Frankfurt am Main, Germany, June 2021

FUT RES
UK

Introduction: Futures in Mind

Life is change. It encompasses many possibilities and great openness to what might come. Fortunately. Otherwise, everything would be predetermined, and we humans would just be the implementing agents of some big plan. Every organization, every society consists of a great variety and number of individuals who see a great number of possibilities and make multiple decisions every day. These individuals have images of possible, probable, and desirable future developments in their minds. Therefore, I use the plural in this book: futures. A lot of people have a lot of ideas about a lot of different futures. In addition, the openness of future developments also means that we should think in multiple futures. Even more, none of those futures will become reality later given complexity and uncertainty.

This book was written for all those who are concerned with the future. Which is basically everyone. Because even when you cross the street, you are dealing with the future. Will the cyclist from the right arrive at a certain point at the same time as you will? Then you should adjust your plan for crossing the street accordingly. You do not need this book for this adjustment.

However, future developments are often not so easy to predict, and it is often not possible to make reliable plans. While we might wish for this certainty and predictability, all too often it is unrealistic. The major upheavals of 2020/21 have made the uncertainty and openness of the future visible to everyone.

Confidently deal with the later-than-now

Even before Covid-19 many people felt overwhelmed by the openness and uncertainty of the later-than-now. This book offers some signposts, backgrounds, experiences, and ideas for action for the confident handling of uncertainty. These ideas should enable the readers to make the various images and assumptions about futures visible and usable in the present. There are many approaches and methods for this. The competency to use these methods for different purposes is called futures literacy. It could be one of the most important competencies of humankind in the 21st century. Just as being able to read and write has been an increasingly important competency since the 19th century.

As humanity, we decided that not just a few people should be able to read and write, but as many as possible. This book is a contribution to enabling as many people as possible to competently deal with the future. Not everyone who can read and write will create poems or a dissertation. However, it has proven to be helpful and important that people can read the newspaper or an instruction manual or write a letter to relatives, for example. The same applies to futures literacy: it is an increasingly important competency for everyone, even if not everybody will be active as a process designer or as an author of research papers. Everyone can use this competency in everyday life. This book offers concrete suggestions for how to do this.

This path towards higher futures literacy will not be an easy one and we are only at the beginning of it. Many people long for the greatest possible stability and security in all areas of life, for certainty in planning. They look for obvious connections between cause and effect. They want clear solutions for big problems, and they want exact answers to their questions. Some leaders in politics, business, the media, and even science promise this clarity, this security. In our modern, complex societies, this is an illusion for many important issues – or it is associated with enormous restrictions to freedom, diversity, and vitality.

Openness and uncertainty as gifts

This book shows another way. It is an invitation to accept the openness and uncertainty of the future as a gift (Roberto Poli) , to discover new possibilities, and to deal with these competently. Even if starting from a deep-seated fear of the future, new hope, new confidence, and new action can emerge. The book is intended to strengthen the understanding of the interrelationships and whet the appetite for action. By applying new ideas ourselves, we learn more intensively and improve our skills. We did not learn to read and write by merely listening to lectures. We did it ourselves. We started small, first with single letters, then words, later whole texts, and at some point fluency was achieved. Futures literacy can be strengthened step by step by our own doing.

Over time, you will be able to experiment with different futures. You will strengthen your imagination, be more innovative. You will also be able to work better with the collective intelligence of your organization. You will develop more powerful questions. You will discover or rediscover the importance of improvisation, spontaneity, and play. You will probably also become more humble, more relaxed, more serene. If you are already doing or can do all this, then hopefully this book will provide you with relevant background and further inspiration. If you longed to do some of these things for some time, this book offers some arguments and many ideas for concrete steps towards more futures work. If you are not able to understand some of the terms mentioned, this is no problem at all. As you learned to read, you did not need to know what an ode or a dissertation is, who Shakespeare or Goethe were, to be able to take your next step.

Two pillars

The book stands on two pillars. Firstly, my own practical experience with major futures processes, which I have advised or organized over the past 10 years. This begins with the process about the future of the social market economy. It continues with my work as a core expert in the Dialogue on Germany's Future of the German Chancellor and on the scientific advisory board of the government strategy "Wellbeing in Germany".

The processes "Positive Futures – Forum for Frankfurt" and #gutlebendigital (Quality of Life in the Digital Age) of the non-profit association Center for Societal Progress (ZGF - Zentrum für gesellschaftlichen Fortschritt) brought further insights. These processes are described in the third part of the book. Through them, I met many wonderful people and learned a lot about content and methods.

The second pillar of the book is the result of the close cooperation with futures experts such as Riel Miller at UNESCO, who is promoting the competency of "Futures Literacy". In his book "Transforming the Future: Anticipation in the 21st Century" I edited the case studies and presented our process in Frankfurt as an extended futures literacy process. Together with Riel, I designed Futures Literacy Laboratories in Dubai and Dublin, co-curated the "UNESCO Global Futures Literacy Design Forum" in Paris in 2019, and helped prepare the "High-Level

Futures Literacy Summit" in late 2020. The insights and experiences from this collaboration are reflected in the book in hopefully easy-to-understand language.

Basis – tools – applications

In its three sections, the book first offers basic considerations, then concrete tools and methods, and finally my own experiences from applications in larger futures processes on wellbeing and quality of life. If you are particularly interested in these applications and results, jump to chapters 16 to 19 and turn later to the more theoretical chapters 1 to 5. If you are looking for useful tools for dealing with your own futures issues, start in the middle section from chapter 6 and then look to the right or left. And, of course, you may also read the book in the sequence it is printed: Basis, Tools, Applications. Each chapter is self-contained and requires no knowledge of the previous chapters. It ends with concrete ideas for the next steps of the readers so that they can actively strengthen their own futures literacy.

My great thanks go to all the people who have shaped and accompanied my path to futures over the past 15 years, who have made the processes and reports possible through their contributions, who have invited me into their processes and events, with whom I have been able to discuss, from whom I have been able to learn, who have allowed my library to grow with their recommendations, who have critically questioned. Some of these people are mentioned in this book. I apologize to all those who are not mentioned by name.

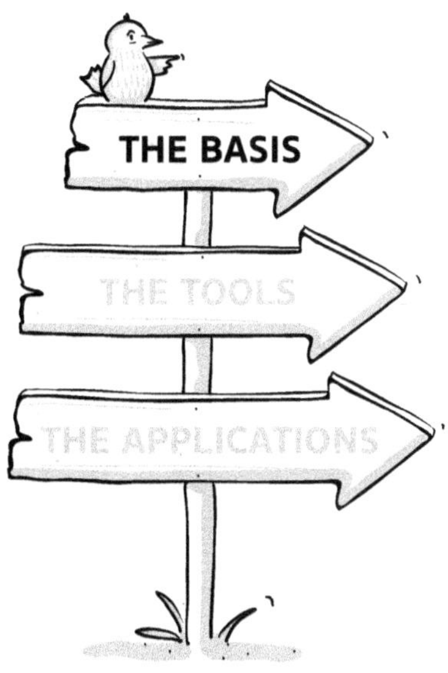
THE BASIS
THE TOOLS
THE APPLICATIONS

 Talking to Each Other - Dialogue

A gray telephone with a turntable, thickly wrapped in a gauze bandage. A cassette player, also wrapped so that the sound is difficult to hear. This is how the artist Barbara Meisner depicts the difficulties of communication in her childhood. Many important topics were hardly spoken about in her family and in Germany in general. These include the traumatic experiences of the baby boomer generation born around 1940, who as small children experienced war, hunger, death, flight, and expulsion in bombed-out cities, in the countryside, or on endless walks westwards. After the war, these "war children" shaped Germany with their experiences.

They built institutions of security and stability, for which we can all be grateful. For some younger people with different backgrounds, however, these institutions appear to be too inflexible today. Most other societies probably have traumas of different kinds, but often with lasting effects as well.

Barbara Meisner showed us in her artistic presentation at a meeting of the "war grandchildren", the children of the war children, how little these traumas were talked about. This made it clear to me why talking to each other is so important to me and why it is sometimes difficult to find the right forums and allies for this. In my youth, I also missed the deep conversation with my family and beyond.

Intensive, trusting conversations

The silence about this traumatic time, also about the guilt and responsibility of the grandparents, has contributed to the fact that we in Germany and probably elsewhere have not experienced and practiced dialogue all that much. By dialogue, I mean an intensive, trusting conversation between people, following the theory and practice developed by Socrates, David Bohm, Martin Buber, and William Isaacs, which leads to a deeper understanding of each other and opens up new possibilities. In my processes over the last years, this dialogue emerged as the basis and starting point for all further steps.

In addition to the traumatic war experience, there are other explanations about why genuine dialogue is not easy in Germany and elsewhere. In recent decades, one scientific discipline has had a particularly strong impact on societies in Germany and worldwide:

economics, the discipline in which I received a diploma and a doctorate. There is no need for dialogue in economics. What is needed is for market participants to make visible their prices, the available quantities, and their qualities. Then everyone puts together the appropriate shopping basket. Money and goods change hands. Done. Those who have sold nothing or too little will leave the market. Those who have sold a lot are likely to raise their prices in the next round or produce more. A dialogue about individual or societal preferences is not necessary. There is no need to talk about desirable futures since in this theory the free market makes peoples' wishes visible.

In this economics-based narrative, the best way into the future is to expand the market to more and more areas: privatization, deregulation, and liberalization. This has been the mantra of a growing number of economists since the 1980s at the latest. As a neoclassically trained economist, I was in the middle of this narrative from 1997 to 2008 at the American investment bank Merrill Lynch and at Deutsche Bank. And I fled because these ideas fall short on many important societal issues.

We cannot let the market alone organize our education system, our democracy, and certainly not our important living together in families, neighborhoods, and cities. The same applies to security, environment, culture, and mobility. All these are among the big, important issues for people's quality of life and the futures of our societies. Without dialogue, we cannot address these issues satisfactorily, we cannot find out what is really important to us as human beings, and therefore where action is needed.

Dialogue and hierarchy

In Germany, another issue makes open, honest dialogue more difficult: hierarchy. Some people do not consider dialogue to be important because they are in a prominent position high up in a hierarchy and can decide on the future. This is where influences from the German Empire until 1918 and the authoritarian regimes up to 1945 or, in the eastern part of Germany, up to 1990 continue to have an effect. These imprints continue, consciously or unconsciously, in companies and political parties. To take this to the extreme: Why talk to the ordinary workers, what do they know? Why stay in touch with the electorate, after they elected me as their representative for five years? Both are attitudes that seem increasingly out of date. But we are not yet used to a different approach, we have not practiced it.

Hierarchical structures are stable when the instructions from above are implemented further down the line. But this is how fewer and fewer employees and citizens want to work today. They see for themselves what works and what doesn't. They have a wealth of experience that is important for the success of an organization and a whole society. These people want to get involved. Of course, this does not mean that everyone should have a say in everything. Children do not learn spelling through dialogue. Facts about climate change are not up for discussion. But the potential of dialogue is far from exhausted.

The art of thinking together

Heiko Roehl opened the door to dialogue for me after he attended the opening ceremony of the Center for Societal Progress in 2009. There I outlined our plans to give the issue of quality of life greater visibility and greater societal relevance in Germany. He then told me: "Stefan, what you have in mind here is a change process at the societal level. Look at the methods that are used at the organizational level to achieve this." He referred me to his book on "Mapping Dialogue" and to the masterminds like David Bohm and William Isaacs mentioned earlier.

For William Isaacs, dialogue is the art of thinking together and having a conversation with a center instead of sides. That is why dialogues are usually held in circles where no one has a special position. Issacs distinguishes dialogue from other forms of conversation. For a competent handling of the future, it is important to know which form one sees or wants to create. Do you want to have a debate (from French débattre, knock down) in which the speakers skillfully put their own point of view into words and defend it? The most applause is given to the more powerful, louder, more eloquent, or even the wittier speaker. One does not listen to understand, but to work on one's counter speech. Places for debate are parliaments, debating clubs, panel discussions, and evening talk shows on television. The roles and the process are clear, but not much new can be created in this way. Besides, you rarely convince your counterpart in such a format anyway. Maybe some of the listeners.

Or do we want a discussion, in which we examine a topic together and perhaps arrive at a synthesis of the original points of view? Then there is more openness to learn something from the other person, at least to acknowledge and consider their arguments and data.

Isaacs is primarily concerned with the possibilities of a reflective and generative dialogue in which new ideas emerge from the collective intelligence of the participants. He wants to investigate the underlying causes, rules, and assumptions of a topic to make deeper questions visible. Isaacs refers to the physicist David Bohm and sees dialogue as an opportunity to think together and thus to do whatever needs to be done in an intelligent way. A central object of investigation in Bohm's dialogue is assumptions, i.e. statements or connections that have not been proven or cannot even be proven. They are made visible and the real or supposed constraints behind them are investigated. These assumptions of the various participants are not judged but are kept in suspense. The aim is to make new meaning visible in the flow of words when all participants investigate the assumptions together.

In this way new things can be created, innovation becomes possible on a solid basis. For Isaacs, the most important results of a conversation are those that none of the participants could have imagined in advance. Of course, it is difficult to determine exactly which part of a conversation is completely new. Afterward, many will think that they had already had that thought years ago or had even written it down somewhere.

Dialogue in practice

Bohm prefers a simple format: participants sit down in a circle, without a facilitator, without an agenda, without a goal, and see what emerges. This is an experiment, an attempt to do something new or different. It is unusual, it can even be frightening. In the beginning, the group will probably remain quite superficial, talking about the format. Then with a little practice, they can gradually go deeper.

As beautiful and important as the generative, reflective dialogue sounds, in practice it is seldomly held like this. Moreover, the term dialogue is now often misused and thus damaged: "dialogue mailings" are advertisements, many dialogue forums are primarily public relations. This is easy to see. But it is difficult to use genuine dialogue in futures processes. In addition to the challenges of lack of practice and hierarchical structures mentioned earlier, there is the fundamental requirement that dialogues should be open regarding the outcome. Only in this way can new things be created. This openness contradicts the widespread pursuit of previously established self-interests. Why should I get involved in dialogue if it is not certain that my viewpoints, my products, or my policies will gain more visibility as a result? Openness and self-interest are not good friends. In complex human systems, it is important to find ways to deal with both.

Initiate a dialogue yourself

For you as the reader, this chapter has probably caused some reflection. Perhaps you already have ideas about how and with whom you can enjoy a more lively or dynamic dialogue in your context. Here are a few suggestions from my side:

Use the arguments in this chapter to seek open, non-hierarchical discussions of relevant issues in the workplace or your organization.

Encourage events in your environment with more dialogue elements to complement the usual lecture formats and panel discussions.

Organize your own salon in the format of a dialogue, whether according to Bohm or Isaacs, or whomever.

In discussions with politicians, point out the importance of ongoing dialogue and suggest topics and formats for it.

Read David Bohm's "On Dialogue" or William Isaac's "Dialogue and the Art of Thinking Together".

2 Ask Powerful Questions

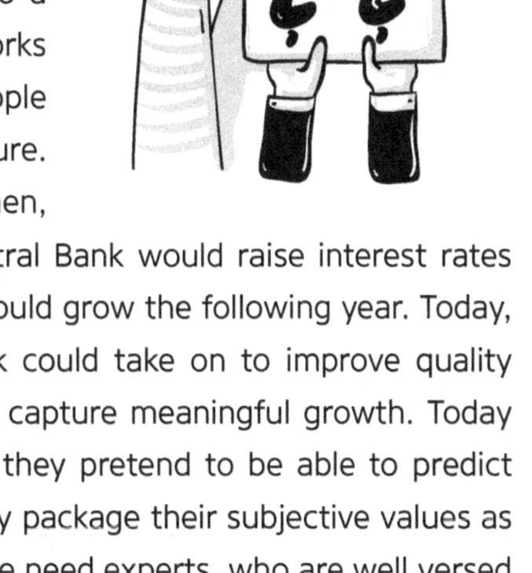

I used to have answers, now I ask questions. This describes my change from an economist, who travels around the world and explains the situation in Europe to clients, to a futurist and facilitator who works together with many other people to develop new ideas for the future. I used to make forecasts about when, for example, the European Central Bank would raise interest rates or how strongly the economy would grow the following year. Today, I ask what tasks a central bank could take on to improve quality of life and which indicators can capture meaningful growth. Today I question forecasters: Why do they pretend to be able to predict the future? Do they perhaps only package their subjective values as objective research? Of course, we need experts, who are well versed in their subject in the present, who are nationally and internationally connected, and who explain their knowledge in a comprehensible way. Their knowledge of numbers, facts, and contexts is and will remain important. But we also need questions.

Every futures process, every dialogue, every event should have a good starting question. Finding such good questions is not difficult if you consider a few points and ask yourself the following questions, based on the work of Eric Vogt, Juanita Brown, and David Isaacs:

1. RELEVANCE:

Is the question relevant to the people who want or should explore it? Is there a relationship between what these people do and what is important to them? On this occasion one can also ask the other way round: For whom is the question relevant as well? Who else should be in the room to explore it?

2. OPENNESS:

Is the answer to the question not yet known? Suggestive questions, in which the desired answer is already more or less well hidden, bring little new insight.

3. EFFECT:

What effect should the question have on the participants? What kind of conversation, reflection, or even feelings could it evoke? Of course, the question should not be too demanding.

4. NOVELTY:

If the same question has been discussed over and over again, then something may have gone wrong. One is going around in circles and might want to look for other questions to break out of the circle.

5. IMPETUS:

Can the question provide the impetus to search for even better, more relevant questions? The opening question should not be carved in stone. If a better question emerges during the discussion - and is accepted as such by the participants - then that question should be pursued.

6. RESULT:

Does the question have the potential to lead to relevant answers that will help us move forward?

Three dimensions of good questions

Questions can also be analyzed along three dimensions. First, the structure of the question: closed yes-no questions are generally less helpful than questions about when and where. Even better are what-questions. Especially powerful are questions about why and how. "Are you satisfied with your working atmosphere?" Participants can answer that question with 'yes' or 'no' or select an answer on a fixed scale from 0 to 10. The knowledge you gain is limited.

"When were you particularly satisfied with your working atmosphere?" This question could be a bit more powerful if the answer is not only "last week" or "last year". It can provide an introduction to a real conversation about when something went well. Even more powerful would be: "What in your working environment makes you particularly satisfied?" Of course, it should not just be a ready-made list to choose from, but the dialogue on different aspects should be encouraged. The following question could be particularly powerful: "Why do you like to be at work on some days and not so much on others?"

The second dimension is the scope of the question. Is it about the working climate in a particular group, in a department, in an organization, or a whole country? It is important to find a good balance between ambition and realism. The group may be too small as a unit of investigation, a country as a whole may be too large. In any case, it would be helpful if the scope of the question were clear in advance.

The third dimension is the assumptions in the question. For example: "How can we strengthen private schools?" This question assumes that all parties have an interest in making private schools stronger. Probably those who do not share this interest will not feel invited. Or: "What is not going well in sales?" is a question with the assumption that there is a problem at a specific point. It can lead to a defensive attitude of the sales department, deepen old ditches and so perhaps the actual issue is overlooked. When a question is formulated, one should therefore be clear about one's values and assumptions that may have been incorporated into it. Then one can try to look at the question from the perspective of a person who has different values and assumptions.

The question behind the question

Many futures methods do not stop at the introductory question but develop deeper questions. In the method of the so-called "Pro-Action Café", for example, it is first discussed in small groups which question, which concern lies behind or below the introductory question. In this way, the assumptions of the questioner are made visible, and alternatives are developed. In the second and third rounds, the alternatives are then analyzed together, and elegant next steps are developed.

In the "Dynamic Facilitation" method, four lists are kept in parallel as the minutes of the discussion. The first list collects facts and information that do not need to be discussed further. The second list contains the solutions and answers to the initial question. The third list records reservations and objections to the proposed solutions. And the fourth list collects new challenges and new, more detailed questions. During the process, the group can decide whether it wants to change the question and discuss solutions to the more important, more relevant question.

In Futures Literacy Laboratories (chapter 12) even more effort is put into finding new questions. Discussions about desirable, probable, and alternative futures lay the foundation for new, deeper questions and appropriate actions.

Also, at the end of dialogue events, I like to ask a question about questions: "Which question do you think has been neglected today?" This tells you first of all whether the initial question of the event has achieved what you had hoped for. And you get a lot of material for possible follow-up events.

Which new questions arise cannot, of course, be determined at the beginning of such a process. This is precisely the added value of questions for dealing with fundamentally open futures. From the point of view of some hosts, this is also a danger. What do we do if new, perhaps unpleasant questions arise for us? How do we react? In my view, such considerations show the added value of an open approach: If the new questions that arise are relevant, then sooner or later they will come up anyway. Every manager and every organization should have an interest in knowing them as early as possible.

Questions in concrete processes

At the beginning of the two-year dialogue process "Positive Futures - Forum for Frankfurt" (chapter 17) we spent a lot of time looking for the best possible questions. They should be relevant to a large number of people. They should be open regarding content, partly because we needed to build legitimacy as neutral organizers of the process. They should stimulate a deeper discussion about quality of life among the participants. In addition, they should be able to provide an impetus for the participants' activities. It should also be possible to harvest the answers so that they could be used for further analysis. We decided on four questions that build on each other.

1. What is important to you personally in your life?

This question was about addressing the participants as human beings and not in a specific position or role. Focusing on the individual and on the here and now was relatively straightforward. During the preparatory work, concerns were expressed as to whether the participants in the dialogues would have answers to such a very personal question and whether they wanted or could express them. All these concerns quickly turned out to be unfounded during the events.

2. What constitutes a high quality of life in Frankfurt?

With this question, the step from the individual to the urban society was taken. This worked quite well, even though the answers to the first question often provided the context for the answers to the second. Here it was important to ask deepening questions in the dialogue events, to get the participants to talk to each other and to let new ideas emerge from the connections.

3. What hurts your heart when you think of Frankfurt?

We had a long and controversial discussion in the project team about this question. The basic idea of "Positive Futures" was to work positively, to make desirable futures visible. And then this negative question. In retrospect, this was the question that made a particularly large number of additional topics visible without causing the mood to flip into the negative. Here everyone had an opinion and was able to share concrete experiences. For the later steps in the process the question posed no problems: It was simply a matter of reducing these negative points.

4. Frankfurt in 15 years: which changes would you like to see?

This is where we wanted to look ahead. The time horizon of 15 years seemed reasonable to us. But this question did not work well. The answers were mainly about having more of what was discussed in question 2 and less of what was discussed in question 3.

Good questions are thus an essential building block for dealing with open futures in complex human systems. In the following chapters, questions will appear again and again as a central theme and additional concrete examples will be given.

Questions to good processes

Organizers of every futures process, every initiative, every event should also be able to answer a whole range of questions in the development phase. The Canadian process facilitator Chris Corrigan has sorted them into eight stages. He starts with the need and asks: What is going on in the world right now that makes our work important? What are the challenges and opportunities we are facing? Why is it important that we do this work? This should then lead to the purpose of the project with further questions: If this work should live up to its fullest potential, what do you imagine is possible? What do we want to stimulate? Once this has been clarified, it is a matter of a jointly developed and shared understanding of the principles of cooperation in the project: How do we want to work with each other and with the participants? What should we always think of when we meet for joint project work?

Fourthly, then about the people who are involved in the project. Who is in the room? Who is not in the room and how could we get them in? Who has an interest in the results of the project? Once these are clarified, the concept of the process can be discussed. What form should our work take? Which form fits the need, the purpose, the principles, and the people?

My favorite level in Corrigan's structure is the sixth, the "limiting beliefs": What makes us tremble, and what do we fear about new ways of working together? What are the cynics and skeptics saying about our work? What questions have we not yet asked ourselves? Then it comes to the concrete structure: How do we decide what to focus time, money, attention, and energy on? How much of it do we need or have? What role does the core team play?

Then it is about the practice of cooperation: Who does the inviting to meetings? Which platforms are used? Finally, it is about the harvest: How should the results be recorded? How can the harvest best serve the purpose of the project? How do we remain open to what may come out of it?

Possibilities for you about questions

Those were many, many questions. They are important questions. They are an invitation for you to focus more on questions. There are a lot of opportunities for that. Among them:

If you participate in events and processes, you can track the initial question and investigate it according to the criteria described above. You may even have the opportunity to suggest an alternative question before or during the event. And you can consider for whom this question is not relevant or who might answer it differently than the people in the room. Perhaps you can even investigate the question behind the question.

As organizers of events and processes, you can use the insights of this chapter to reflect on your question and perhaps formulate more powerful questions. And you can try to bring more of the groups into the room that might also have a connection to this question.

If you would like to take a closer look at the sources mentioned above: The article by Vogt, Brown, and Isaacs from 2003 is entitled "The Art of Powerful Questions" and is easy to find on the Internet. The many questions

by Chris Corrigan are taken from his "Chaordic Stepping Stones", of which there are now variations in different lengths.

There is a short overview of the "Pro Action Café" by Amanda Fenton. For Dynamic Facilitation, there is English material available from Jim Rough.

 Dealing with Complexity

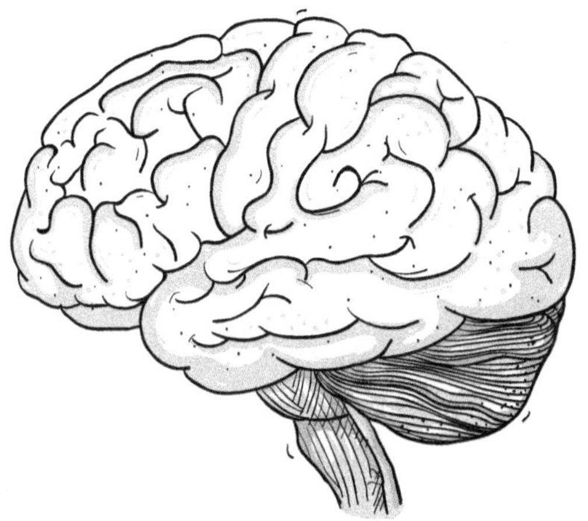

Spring 2005 on the campus of the Catholic University of Leuven. I am waiting in line for the bus that will take the participants of the Millennium Project's futurist conference to the historic castle of Corroy for dinner. The friendly person from Finland next to me asks me how I take emergence, non-linearities, and the final causes of complex systems into account in my forecasting models for Deutsche Bank. I tried in vain to understand what he was trying to tell me and why it might have any relevance for me. That evening marked the beginning of my wonderfully helpful learning journey into complexity theory and methods for a higher quality of life that do justice to societal complexity as much as possible. The friendly Finn was Mika Aaltonen, a trained economist, and former professional soccer player. Since then, he has connected me with many other people and ideas from the world of complexity that are important for futures work.

Clear, complicated, complex, or chaotic

My journey into the world of complexity theory continued with the fundamental distinction between clear, complicated, complex, and chaotic systems. A system consists of several elements that are in certain relationships with each other. The Welsh complexity expert David Snowden illustrates this in his Cynefin model. He emphasizes time and again that each of these systems requires a different approach.

Clear systems are – clearly simple. Everyone understands them, there are clear connections between cause and effect. Opening a door is possible for everyone: apply the handle, move the door, walk through. Many processes in the business world, such as changes of address or packaging goods, belong here. For them, there is a best practice, central guidelines, and great potential for automation. However, these systems are not entirely without their dangers. It may be that the head office of a large organization only sets guidelines and does not notice enough what is happening on site. This makes it difficult for them to react to changes in the environment. There ought to be a way to get new, possibly unpleasant information to the head office even in clear systems, as they may change over time.

The mechanics of complicated systems

Complicated systems are something for experts. Here too, there are clear connections between cause and effect, but these can only be understood by people with the appropriate specialist knowledge. Only car mechanics can recognize exactly where the problem of a broken car engine lies - and fix it if possible. The physicist Isaac Newton was the mastermind of this linear approach. The engineer Frederick Winslow Taylor anchored it industrially with the assembly production line at Ford car manufacturing. Even in complicated systems, there are sometimes different ways to solve a problem. All these ways have their advantages and disadvantages in terms of cost and benefit. There is no longer only one best practice as in clear systems, but often several good practices. Even in complicated systems, dangers are lurking. One of these dangers is analysis paralysis: experts analyze, analyze, and analyze. They get stuck and cannot agree on a solution because everyone wants to be the winner of the argument. Also, it could be that non-experts with a fresh view have innovative ideas that the experts do not take into account.

The relevance of complex systems

Complex systems are particularly relevant to approaching open futures. They are systems with many interacting elements that can develop jointly, dynamically, non-linearly, and unpredictably, and in doing so can give rise to something new. These systems cannot be disassembled into their parts like a car engine and reassembled later without a loss. The whole is much more than the sum of the individual parts. Forests are complex, adaptive, emergent systems. Brains are too. All human systems are. There are no best or even several good solutions to important questions. Sometimes patterns can be seen where experts can help.

In such cases, experiments are useful and may bring the system one step forward. Ideally, those should be experiments that can be terminated without dramatic consequences if they show undesirable results: safe to fail. When dealing with complex systems, discussions must be opened up as much as possible. The variety of perspectives must be increased, contradictions allowed, dialogue must be made possible. A fertile ground should be prepared on which new things can be created - without knowing in advance what exactly this might be.

Chaotic systems are for strong, decisive leaders. There is no time and no place here for long analysis, questioning, or trial and error. No one knows which cause can lead to which effect. Somebody needs to decide and act quickly. After the crisis, the heroes who have overcome it can be celebrated. The danger for managers is that later they will not get out of the crisis mode and the heroic role of the chaotic system and find their way back into the appropriate leadership role for complex or complicated systems. Fortunately, chaotic systems or times are rather rare. Other times require a different kind of leadership.

In many countries, thinking in terms of complicated systems still seems to dominate. Expert opinions are in demand, external consultants are called in, commissions are convened, decisions are made - and later one often wonders why the hoped-for result does not materialize. Why this fixation on complicated systems? It is possible that classical engineering countries are particularly good at improving engines and machines, but don't want to focus on complexity. Or the limit may lie in hierarchical structures of societies, where you wait for instructions from superiors or experts.

Futures methods for complex systems

The friendly Finn from the beginning of this chapter, Mika Aaltonen, had examined many methods of futures research to see if they are appropriate for complex societal systems. He was looking for methods that, firstly, do not attempt to establish clear rules for controlling the system. That would be appropriate for simple systems. Rather, he was more interested in methods that allow ambiguity of results where there are, at first glance, no clear right or wrong answers. In this way, one does justice to the openness of the future. Secondly, it should be methods that do not try to understand the system only from the outside through the expert's perspective but work in interaction with the parts of the system. He rarely found this combination of "ambiguity and interaction with the system". In his opinion, most futures methods are engineering methods: the analysts look at the system from the outside and search for regularities to derive recommendations for the decision-makers. Horizon scanning, trend maps, and forecasting models are among them for him.

Although many other methods allow ambiguity, the analysts are also outside the system. Among these methods of systemic thinking, he includes Delphis, prediction markets, or robust decision making. Scenarios can be created with or without ambiguity, depending on the approach. Only Causal Layered Analysis, participatory methods, and visioning processes met Mika's high standards. I would add Future Search and Futures Literacy Laboratories. These are the methods I have been working with over the past ten years and they are highlighted in this book. They aim to do justice to the complexity of modern societies and take into account emergence and non-linearities.

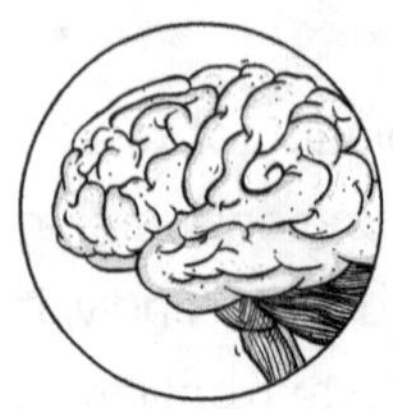

The systems you are in

A next step for you could be to become more aware of the type of system in which your future issues are located. Presumably, these will be complicated or complex systems.

Discuss details, differences, procedures with your team. You could also look for examples where questions from complex systems were answered with the toolbox of complicated systems. As a bonus, you could discuss possible undesirable consequences of this approach with colleagues.

For further reading, I recommend David Snowden's article with Mary Boone in the Harvard Business Review "A Leader's Framework for Decision-Making" from 2007, which describes the Cynefin Model. Mika Aaltonen's book "Complexity as a Sensemaking Framework" from 2005 also includes guest contributions from other complexity researchers. Paul Cilliers goes even deeper in his 1998 book "Complexity & Postmodernism - Understanding Complex Systems".

4 Involve Many Different People

A spring evening in the German Federal Chancellery in 2013. Ahead of the first International German Forum on "What matters to people - wellbeing and progress", the speakers meet the Chancellor's team for dinner. Next to me sits Ben Warner from Jacksonville, the largest city of Florida, where he ran a process to improve quality of life over many years with great success. At the Center for Societal Progress, we had written a research report on his indicator process and I had the pleasure of recommending him as a speaker for the Forum. Now we are meeting for the first time in person, and I am telling him about ideas for an indicator process in Frankfurt am Main based on his process in Jacksonville.

From the following conversation I took his strong message with me: "Stefan, if you want to run a solid process on quality of life, then try to involve as many different people as possible. If you have 100 people in the process, then every person in your city should feel understood by at least one of those people." This was the high standard he always aimed for in Jacksonville. His statement did not let me go since then.

A tall order

All the futures processes I was involved in later were to include as many different perspectives as possible. They should not remain trapped in filter bubbles of people with similar thoughts, who then wonder why the results of their process are hardly used by others.

Rather, they should actively approach people who are not usually heard - the "seldom-heard voices". In companies, these could be team assistants. They are aware of much of what is happening but often have little opportunity to contribute their insights into the decision process. In cities, these may be people in the outer districts, people with lower education, lower income, unusual working hours, or additional burdens of raising children or caring for the elderly.

Such an active approach of the seldom-heard voices by going to where they are, strengthens the democratic legitimacy of all processes, whether they take place at the city level, in companies, or civil society organizations. Democracy is not just about making a cross on a big piece of paper every few years and leaving everything else to the elected representatives. This approach has become less and less effective in recent years, as voter turnout has fallen especially among socially weaker citizens and among people with a history of migration. Democracy also should not consist of letting a small group of educated, older people with similar socialization, work out new proposals on societal issues in special committees. In a democracy, the aspiration should be the equal participation of as many people as possible. In companies, this is subject to tighter limits set by ownership structures.

Meaningful participation

The important thing is that participation should also be seen as making a difference, as contributing to change. It should be "meaningful", as political scientist Brigitte Geißel calls it at her research center for democratic innovations. Participation should not just exist to generate nice photos for an annual report. The results should not disappear in a drawer but should be made visible. Otherwise, the frustration of the people who took part and whose hope for improvement had increased will continue to grow. That applies to democracy as much as it does to business. Of course, it is perfectly acceptable that decision-makers do not implement all the results of a participatory process. That is rarely possible. However, they should argue why they prefer one option over another or even chose none of them. Reasons may include an expert judgment that considers some proposals to be objectively impossible to implement, or simply because there is a lack of money, so priorities must be set.

When equal participation is well done, satisfaction with democracy generally increases. The participants leave the process with a better understanding of other people's perspectives, of the connections between different issues, and of how politics and administration work. The same can apply to companies.

So Ben Warner's message is based on a solid foundation of research into democratic innovation. And it fits with the insights of complexity research: an open dialogue, a high diversity of participants, and the ability to allow disagreement are important. This makes it easier for the underlying patterns to become visible and new ideas to emerge in complex, adaptive systems.

Deal with variety in a fruitful way

An important futures competency is therefore the fruitful dealing with variety, the openness to variety. Not only in daily life, but especially in processes in which societal futures are discussed. Different perspectives and experiences should be heard in the process. There is no guarantee that each insight can be accurately reflected in the final results. But everybody can bring in their pieces of the puzzle, connect them to the other pieces and possibly adapt them considering the overall view. Disappointments cannot be ruled out.

Two issues are important for the designers and facilitators of such a process: First, the different perspectives should be given space and made visible. And secondly, they should be fruitfully connected. That sounds easier than it is. Getting all the different people in the same room at the same time will hardly work. It requires many small opportunities. Also, the differences between people are often quite large: some want to discuss the big philosophical questions, others want to move forward with concrete projects.

The process designer then looks for ways to make cross-fertilization possible nevertheless. This can be done via feedback loops ("What has been said elsewhere") or via groups on individual topics. Again, a good measure of variety or heterogeneity must be found. If, for example, only architects and project developers discuss the topic of "housing", there is a danger that impulses from experts on transport or health issues, on environmental issues, or from the retail sector will not be taken into account. Each topic area, each process has its "seldom-heard voices", which can contribute new perspectives and suggestions. They should not be deterred by a discussion among experts.

Variety in Frankfurt

When we began to put Ben Warner's message into practice in Frankfurt am Main ourselves for the first time, there were some concerns and reservations. Would "these" people have anything substantial to say about quality of life? Would they be able to express their thoughts in a way that we could understand? Both concerns were dispelled with the first small events in an Islamic cultural association and an initiative for long-term unemployed women. What a wealth of thoughts became visible to us there! And even more: How grateful people were that someone came and listened to them, had a clear interest in their topics. All it needed was a safe space, some time, and good questions on a relevant topic. Another concern was justified, however: Isn't it very time-consuming to approach these seldom-heard voices and set up meetings? Yes, it is elaborate.

The first thing to do is to build trust: The purpose of the process and the meeting has to be clarified. This works best if you find the bridge-builders from within your network, who then make the contacts. This is how trust is passed on, this is how doors are opened. I was later able to incorporate these experiences from Frankfurt into the government strategy "Wellbeing in Germany". There, the term "difficult-to-reach groups" was used, which is probably appropriate from the point of view of process designers and the organizers given the effort required for engaging these groups. My hope for the future is that more and more people will have more and more practice interacting with different groups. In this way, these groups will be reached more easily and heard more often. As a result, democracy becomes more alive and the collective intelligence on important societal issues is strengthened.

Seek out the seldom-heard voices

You can also become active here. In every project you are involved in or read about, you can ask:

> **Who is involved here? Is it those who always come, who are always asked? Or has everything been tried to bring together the greatest possible variety of perspectives? Have "seldom-heard voices" been actively approached? Who are these groups and how could one approach them?**

In my seminars at the University of St. Gallen, in Helsinki and in the training courses at the Federal Academy for Security Policy in Berlin, I regularly invited participants to first draw up lists of groups that were not heard so often and then to develop strategies to integrate one of these groups into the respective vision or scenario processes. Many of the participants became aware of the narrow circles in which they usually move and the responsibility they bear to enlarge those circles at least temporarily.

5 Consider Different Systems

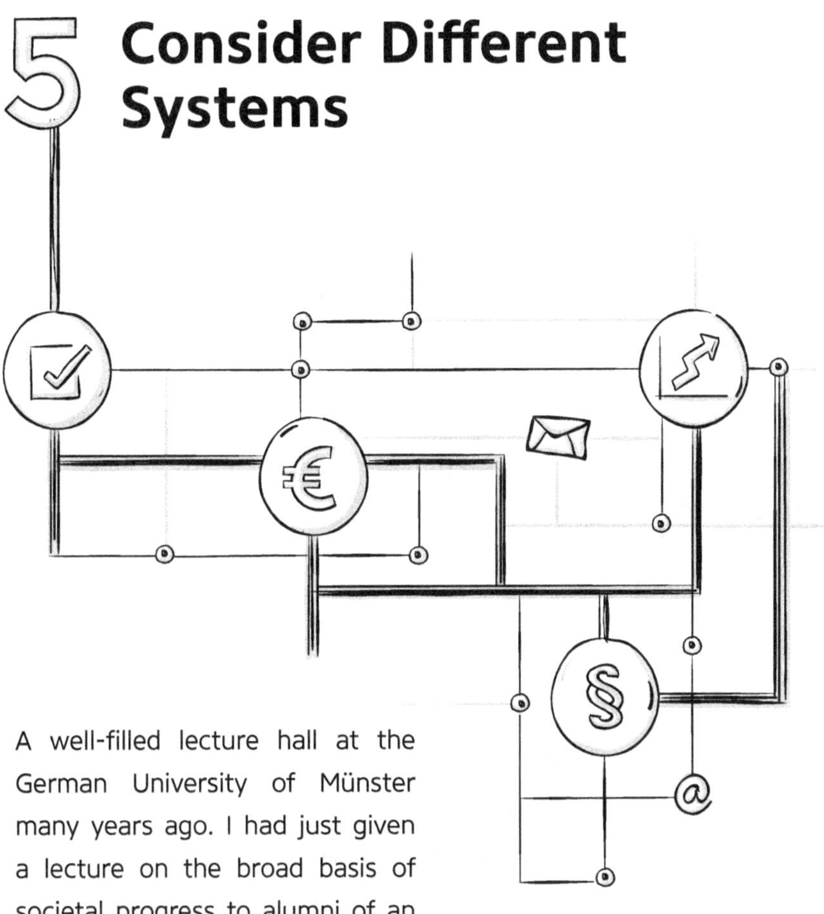

A well-filled lecture hall at the German University of Münster many years ago. I had just given a lecture on the broad basis of societal progress to alumni of an economics institute. Then I was asked how I define society: In the sense of the sociologist Niklas Luhmann as the special social system that includes all communication? At the time, I did not know what the friendly gentleman meant and what he was trying to get at. But I took the question as an opportunity to take a close look at Luhmann and his systems theory afterward and found his ideas increasingly helpful for my work. They allowed me to better understand what was happening in and around my processes.

I apologize to all Luhmann experts for the following presentation of some of his ideas through my perspective and with my words. To all others, I hope to be able to pass on a part of the impulse that was given to me in Münster. This might be especially valuable to all those who do not speak German, as Luhmann's work did not spread much into the English-speaking world. Over time, I recognized many connections between Luhmann and the ideas the Chilean biologist and philosopher Humerto Maturana developed with Francisco Varela, dealing with living systems as autonomous dynamic units. Maturana inspired not only Luhmann but also the American biologist Robert Rosen, who in turn developed the theory of anticipatory systems, to which large parts of futures research refer today.

Connect variety

The basis of all considerations is that complexity results from the combination of several elements in a system. The more elements there are, the higher is the number of possible connections. The number of connections increases exponentially with the number of elements and with it the complexity of the system. At some point, not every element can be linked directly to every other element. It needs to choose with whom direct communication takes place and with whom not. Boundaries are drawn. System boundaries. They must be drawn to avoid overwhelming individual elements and at the same time to be able to handle the variety of the overall system reasonably well. This reduces the complexity for the individual elements. Sub-systems, specializations, and silos develop.

In Luhmann's sense, social systems are autopoietic, self-referential structures that can be described as distinct from their environment.

The important subsystems of society are politics, business, science, law, religion, education, and families. Luhmann's observation that the subsystems develop special communication media, their specific logics and languages, is particularly important for the broad examination of futures. In the political system, power is the decisive medium of communication. With power, you can make others do what you want them to do. In the economy, money is used to communicate, scarce resources are distributed. The subsystem of science is about truth: hypotheses are made, tested, and then evaluated as true or false, right or wrong. The subsystem of law is about whether applicable norms and rules have been observed. Religion refers to the distinction between what is observable and what cannot be observed. And education strengthens people's ability to participate in communication in the first place.

So, if you try to bring together different subsystems in futures processes, some challenges arise through the lens of this systems theory. Why should actors from politics, business, or science get involved in an open process in which it is not clear how this will increase power, money, or truth? In the logic of systems theory, people always act through their roles. A role summarizes the expectations that a social subsystem or an organization has of the holder of a certain position or job. This role description or function is not bound to a specific person. People are therefore bearers of roles in their respective systems and represent them to the outside world accordingly.

Dialogue, roles, and interviews

Of course, these roles, which are enormously important for the functioning of society, make a societal dialogue about futures considerably more difficult. If dialogue aims to create something new, to open to the perspectives and assumptions of the other participants, then that is effectively impossible from a systems theory perspective. In such as setting, a participant must not appear in his or her role and articulate what fits that role. However, a politician, a manager, a scientist cannot communicate unconditionally, as Michael Rautenberg puts it in his book on dialogue in management and organization. This also applies to representatives of individual parties, individual ministries, individual companies, individual departments in a company, or individual scientific disciplines. Making the collective intelligence of the entire system visible is thus basically impossible according to Luhmann's systems theory. In practice, there fortunately are ways to make this work nevertheless.

In recent years, one path has proved to be particularly helpful for me to find out about people's individual perspectives despite the restrictions set by their roles: confidential individual interviews. It has always amazed and delighted me how grateful people are when they can put aside the restrictions imposed by their role and can express themselves as a person confidentially on a relevant topic. Individual interviews are different from dialogue in large groups, where the impulses jump back and forth between the participants and can be further developed by them. In one-on-one conversations, this kind of stimulation can at most be provided by the interviewer through asking questions. However, interviewers must not influence the content of the conversation too much.

Host open to the outcomes

Systems theory also has sobering consequences for the important role of hosts in open dialogue processes: To expect a pharmaceutical company to be the host of an open dialogue process on the future of the healthcare system is, according to systems theory, an illusion. Similarly, it is theoretically impossible for a politician of one party to be the host of a comprehensive dialogue process in which politicians and supporters of other parties participate as individuals.

At the same time, it would also be important from a systems theory point of view if meaning within the individual systems became visible and values in the overall system were clear, and if the various systems retained their structural coupling with the other systems. Let me explain those two points:

Meaning is an achievement of social systems. In biological systems like a jungle, meaning is not an issue. Within a social system, meaning enables self-reference despite a growing number of elements as it enables the individual elements to connect to their system. This meaning is created through experience and communication. In a system with a large number of elements, however, it is not clear whether everyone recognizes a common meaning that helps maintain the system. Values are even broader. They provide a common basis for communication in society and are shared by all. Values are more general than the concrete communication media of power, money, or truth. As a rule, values are quite general, such as peace, freedom, equality, or solidarity. How exactly they are interpreted and how they can be achieved is less clear. There can be different perspectives. Futures processes are precisely about making this variety of perspectives and assumptions visible. They are about negotiating meaning and values.

Signals from the environment

Every system always has a connection to its environment. In Luhmann's terminology, these are structural couplings. The individual system thus recognizes which conditions prevail in its environment, which possibilities result from them, or what it must adapt to. Changes in the environment act as irritations in the respective system and are processed in it. The big question is how these signals are transmitted and how knowledge about the environment is built up. This can happen through crises and shocks. Or through creeping changes in the way the environment acts. In my view, it would be desirable for the signals from the environment to be transmitted in dialogue at an early stage so that some crises and shocks can be avoided or at least one can better prepare for them. This wish comes up against the above-mentioned system-theoretical challenges, starting with the question of who should take the time to do this and why.

To know these challenges and to take them into account in the design of futures processes is, in my opinion, of enormous importance. The alternatives seem less attractive to me: Either each system works by itself and perceives changes in its environment only the hard way and late. Or the systems try to transfer their logic and communication media to the others and thus make them part of their system. If, for example, the economy's money would become the decisive medium also in politics and science, then variety and communication in the overall system will decrease. Or if the power of politics also determines decisions in business and science, then important means of communication are missing.

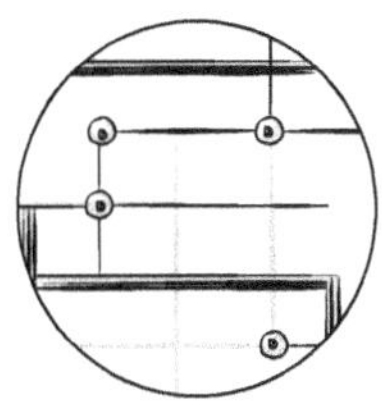

A wise approach to futures work

This chapter is intended to encourage you to work as wisely as possible on your futures project, now that you know the characteristics of complex systems. You better understand the limits of your system, see the importance of roles more clearly and try to deal with them fruitfully. The following chapters provide you with tools for this and show practical examples.

For more details, you may want to read Luhmann's "Theory of Society", which is one of his few books translated into English. Or Christian Borch's 2011 portrait "Niklas Luhmann". Or the introductory 2016 article by Mathias Albert "Luhmann and Systems Theory".

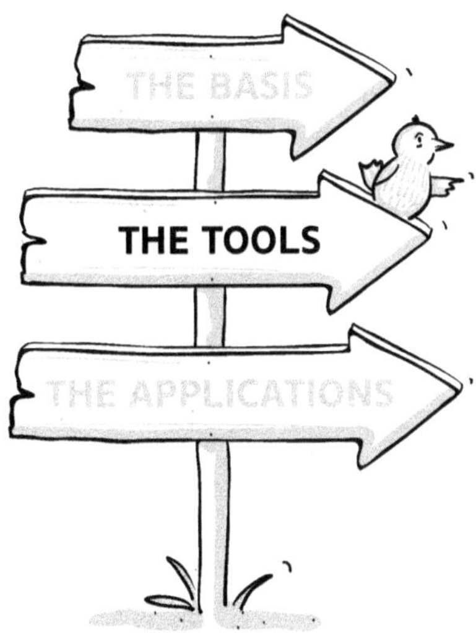

THE BASIS
THE TOOLS
THE APPLICATIONS

6 The Trend May Be Your Friend

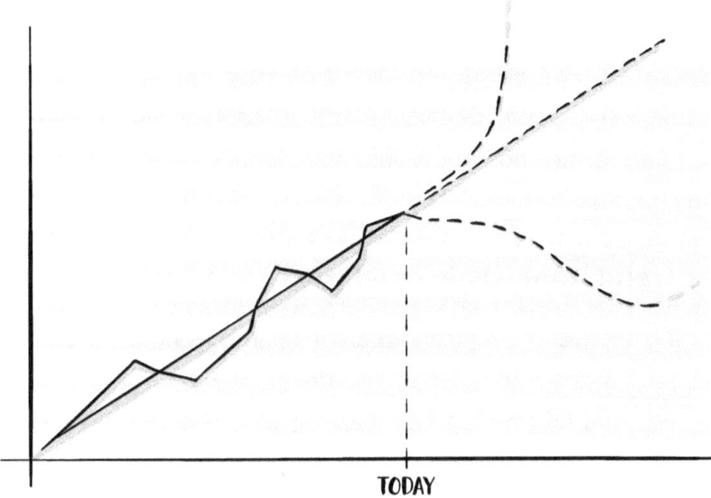

The trend is your friend. That was one of the first rules I learned as an analyst in the banking industry in the mid-1990s. What it meant is that if a stock or an entire market has been moving upwards for some time, then you should go along with this movement and invest. If interest rates have been falling for some time, then you should bet on a further decline. Often this rule has worked well, but often it has not. During my years in the financial industry, one surprise followed the other. For example, after a long period of rapid income growth the Asian crisis in 1997/98, caused worldwide turmoil in the financial markets and severe distortions in the countries affected. But things had been going so well for so long before that! Russia was dragged into the maelstrom in 1998 and devalued the Ruble by 60%. The subsequent political upheavals were massive. In March 2000, the trend of rising share prices of internet companies ended abruptly, which was later called the dotcom bubble. In 2007, the real estate crisis in the United States followed, after prices had been on the rise for so long. The list could be continued at will. One thing is clear: At some point, the trend may no longer be your friend. Can we know when that will happen? Or can we at least protect ourselves in case it ends? Can we position ourselves robust enough so that we do well in many possible futures?

What trend analysis is used for

Describing and discussing trends can be an important contribution to the wise use of the future. Good researchers of the future know what trends are used for and how they are applied in their work. Usually, trends are only one building block, a relatively easily accessible component of this work. In my view, there are at least three reasons to use trends.

Firstly, trends can be used to highlight issues that are important to you personally or to your organization. In this way, attention can be focused, the actions of others can be initiated, and resources can be directed towards a specific area. In the 1980s, for example, these motives were used to make visible the trend of an ever-larger hole in the ozone layer in the southern hemisphere, including the resulting increase in skin cancer. With success. In 1987, the international community agreed to ban the use of chlorofluorocarbons (CFCs) as a refrigerant, because scientists had identified them as the cause of the hole in the ozone layer.

A current example is the upward trend of the earth's temperature, which is being made more visible and should encourage appropriate action. In the financial markets, products that bet on trends are offered daily. But nowadays, such investment products are being given the state-imposed warning that past successes are not a reliable indicator of future performance. One should therefore always ask what interests lie behind the presentation of a specific trend and of the forecast that is often associated with it.

Secondly, trend analysis strengthens the information basis for further discussion and encourages the next steps. Why was this trend selected? What are the reasons behind the trend? Why does it even exist? What connections are there to other trends? What new questions arise from the discussion? Every futures researcher can and should ask such questions, whether in a private, business, or social context. In every futures project, there should be time for such questions. In the method of Future Search (chapter 10), for example, this is the case during the discussion about the present, after the major events of the past had been made visible.

Thirdly, trends can be used to forecast future developments to orientate one's actions accordingly. This works especially well when the future is either near or when past developments have been quite stable. When we cross a road, we always make forecasts about the behavior of other road users. Based on our experience we are quite sure that the cyclist 50 meters away will not be with us in two seconds. But what if it is an e-bike? It is helpful for life insurance companies that in many countries life expectancy is increasing quite steadily by 2.5 years every decade. Therefore, they can calculate future payouts and today's premiums accordingly. Again, there is no such thing as one hundred percent certainty. Russia, the USA, and South Africa are countries where life expectancy fell for some years due to alcohol, drugs, or AIDS. A third example: For central banks and governments, a forecast of economic growth using past trends is indispensable because inflation expectations and tax revenues can be derived from them. Such data is essential for setting interest rates and drawing up budgets for the following year. This is also true even if everybody knows that inflation and tax revenues may, for many reasons, develop differently from forecasts. The year 2020, with the wide variety of responses to the corona pandemic, is an extreme case for a general point.

Properties and requirements

Statistically, a trend is a directional change in a particular variable. This means that each trend is associated with a direction. Something increases or decreases. Otherwise, it would be a constant, a cycle, or just noise. This direction should be visible from every trend title or at the latest from its description. The word "terrorism" is not a trend. Only the "increase in terrorism" indicates the trend.

Moreover, every trend should also be accompanied by solid evidence of its existence. As a rule, these are time series for one or several important aspects of the trend. To stay with the unpleasant subject of the "increase in terrorism": What exactly should and can be proven? An increase in the number of terrorist attacks? Worldwide or in a specific country? Or is it about the number of people killed and injured by the attacks? How exactly is "terrorism" defined? Where is the distinction between this and (civil) war? One can see that important questions arise already in the definition and measurement of a trend. Every user of trends should ask such questions and they bring valuable insights into every futures project.

One of the aims of trend analysis is to broaden the information base for further discussions. It is therefore important that the fundamental causes and drivers of each trend are identified. Again, the unpleasant example of the increase in terrorism: Why do more people resort to violence? Is it a result of poverty? Are there international power struggles behind it? With these questions, one is in the middle of the discussion about systemic causes, about narratives, and perhaps also about myths and metaphors, which will be discussed in chapter 11.

Many important trends

The trend towards more trends began at the latest with John Naisbitt's book "Megatrends" in 1982, where he showed the broad and global impact some trends can have: megatrends. Since then, trend databases, trend conferences, and trend analyses have sprung up around the globe. The variety of sources is too great to do justice to it here. A brief mention should be made of the "Global Trends" published every four years since 1997 by the US government's National Intelligence Council. The British futurist Richard Watson regularly produces maps with hundreds of trends, which are intended to stimulate discussion about current events and possible future developments. The Competence Center Foresight of the German Fraunhofer Institute for Systems and Innovation Research publishes a large number of trend profiles as part of its work in larger futures processes.

Five concrete examples may illustrate the possibilities and limits of trend analysis for dealing with open futures.

Example trend 1: "Incomes are rising". This is an old trend that can be traced back, with interruptions due to recessions and wars, to the beginning of the industrial revolution. As a rule, income per inhabitant is used as the data basis. Among the causes of the trend are the increasing division of labor and the better education of people. Whether the trend will continue in this way is an open question. Perhaps it is weakening because consumption is reaching the limits of the carrying capacity of people and planet. Or because more and more negative effects of globalization are becoming visible, and the international division of labor may not continue as quickly as in the past. Or the trend is being reinforced by technological innovations. We do not know.

Despite the resilience and demonstrability of the trend, it is still unclear what we should do with it. Is the information provided by the trend sufficient to investigate the important issues of our time? Is a general average of income across all people in the country even relevant? Shouldn't we better use the "median equivalized income", i.e. take into account that people living alone need more income than multi-person households, and should we concentrate on the people in the middle of that income distribution? Or do we need separate income data for the top and bottom 10% of the population? Is income the correct measure at all, or should we not better consider wealth? Questions upon questions, as soon as you take a closer look at a trend.

Example trend 2: "Life expectancy is rising". Here the formulation of the trend title is already important. In this example, it does not say

"aging of society" or "people are getting older and older". The reason for this is the unclear and subjective definition of "old", which can also change over time ("60 is the new 50"). Fortunately, the average life expectancy of people at a certain age can be clearly defined and measured – assuming past trends continue. Another nice thing about this trend is that there are clear causes, especially ever-improving health care. It is also helpful that the increase has been quite stable over the past decades in most countries, which suggests that it may continue.

But then the questions about this trend start: What do we do with the information that people are living longer and longer? Who lives particularly long? Is there a correlation between life expectancy and the levels of education or income? What does all this mean for state pension provision? How do we define "old"? Does it make sense to speak of a "working-age population aged up to 65", or should "working-age" not be defined in a more flexible and individualized way? What does this trend mean for health care provision? For the education system? Questions upon questions, even though this trend has been around for a long time, is stable and is likely to continue. Some of these powerful questions can be answered with more detailed data and by experts. Others should be negotiated in the broadest possible societal dialogue. The trend then "only" provides a data basis for negotiating desirable futures and seeking a common basis for action.

Example trend 3: "Urbanization". In this case, one word is enough to describe a trend. More and more people are moving to cities. It is easy to find indicators for this: For example, the percentage of the population living in cities with more than 100,000 inhabitants. But when searching for the causes, it starts to get difficult. In the Middle Ages, it was said that "city air makes you free". There is probably still something to this today. Concrete causes for urbanization in recent years could be the improved air quality in big western cities - compared to the 1960s and 70s. Or the poor supply of broadband internet connections in rural areas. The increasing academization and thus the influx of students to university cities may also be supportive. This list can be continued. Scientific studies have analyzed the individual push and pull factors in detail.

Importantly, it is not clear whether this trend will continue, especially after the experience of the recent pandemic. Overcrowded parks, schools, streets, or subways together with high rents in the big cities may lead to an end of this trend. It is possible that politicians will decide in favor of a nationwide broadband expansion to rural areas as well, and for more intensive promotion of public transport and social infrastructure in rural areas. Here again, observing a trend is the starting point for further questions. Some of these questions can be answered clearly by scientists, others should be addressed in a societal dialogue. Presumably, further questions and hopefully also new solutions for new futures will emerge from the dialogue.

Example trend 4: "The diversity of the population is increasing". In this trend title, various aspects are combined to form a stronger, broader trend. It is presumably about the measurable increase in the proportion of the population with a migration background or also about the less easily measurable differentiation of lifestyles, professions, clothing preferences, or entertainment habits. In the theory of evolution and complexity, this is an unsurprising trend, since higher development is regularly accompanied by more diversity and variety. This trend stimulates a long list of questions as well: How do we deal with increasing diversity? What skills are needed to do so? Or do we not need such competencies since everyone is on their own anyway? Is everyone on their own? What assumptions do we make about others? Is diversity good for us, for us as individuals, and for our society? If not, why not? Should we re-adjust the limits of diversity in clothing styles, public behavior, or even the way we raise children? The answers to these questions reveal different worldviews, ideas of successful futures, and narratives. Here, too, a dialogue is a suitable format for exploring these questions.

Example trend 5: "Environmental issues are becoming more important". This is an intentionally imprecise title to point out traps in the formulation of trends. The environmental issues could be the water quality of rivers, the air quality in cities, the amount of waste, biodiversity, or the temperature of the earth. Or all these together. The first two issues were probably at least as important in the 1960s in Europe as they are today. So where is the trend? It is also not clear whether "more important" refers to absolute or relative assessments in opinion polls or concrete action. Perhaps it also refers to the number of legislative proposals on environmental issues. At the moment, the easiest way to prove the trend is probably to show that, according to surveys, the issue of climate change is becoming increasingly important to people. Again, this is where the questions begin. Try to formulate some yourself!

Trend analysis gets more exciting when we also look at the links between the various trends. Clearly, the trend of rising income has an impact on resource consumption and thus on environmental issues. In the future, environmental issues could also have an impact on economic growth. The direction of these effects can be discussed at length. Or consider diversity and income: It is often pointed out that a high degree of variety goes hand in hand with greater innovation and economic success.

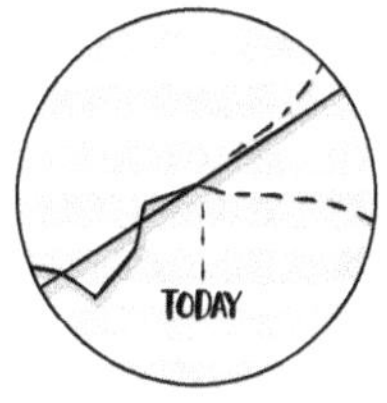

Make friends with trends

People with high futures literacy use trends and question why and how these trends are described and what they are used for. They develop powerful, deeper questions from the trend analysis. I invite you to train in this aspect of futures literacy.

> **Pick one or more (mega)trends from an internet research. Question what exactly the trend is, whether the title is well chosen. Question how well the trend is documented, what the causes could be, what the consequences might be. Which deeper questions arise? Talk about them with other people. Or even develop the trend into a question for a dialogue salon as described in the first and second chapters.**

Or first, delve into the 60 trend profiles on societal change in 2030 that the Fraunhofer Institute had compiled for the German Federal Ministry of Education and Research. The above-mentioned trend map by Richard Watson "Mega Trends and Technologies" is freely accessible via nowandnext.com - and hopefully stimulates intensive discussions.

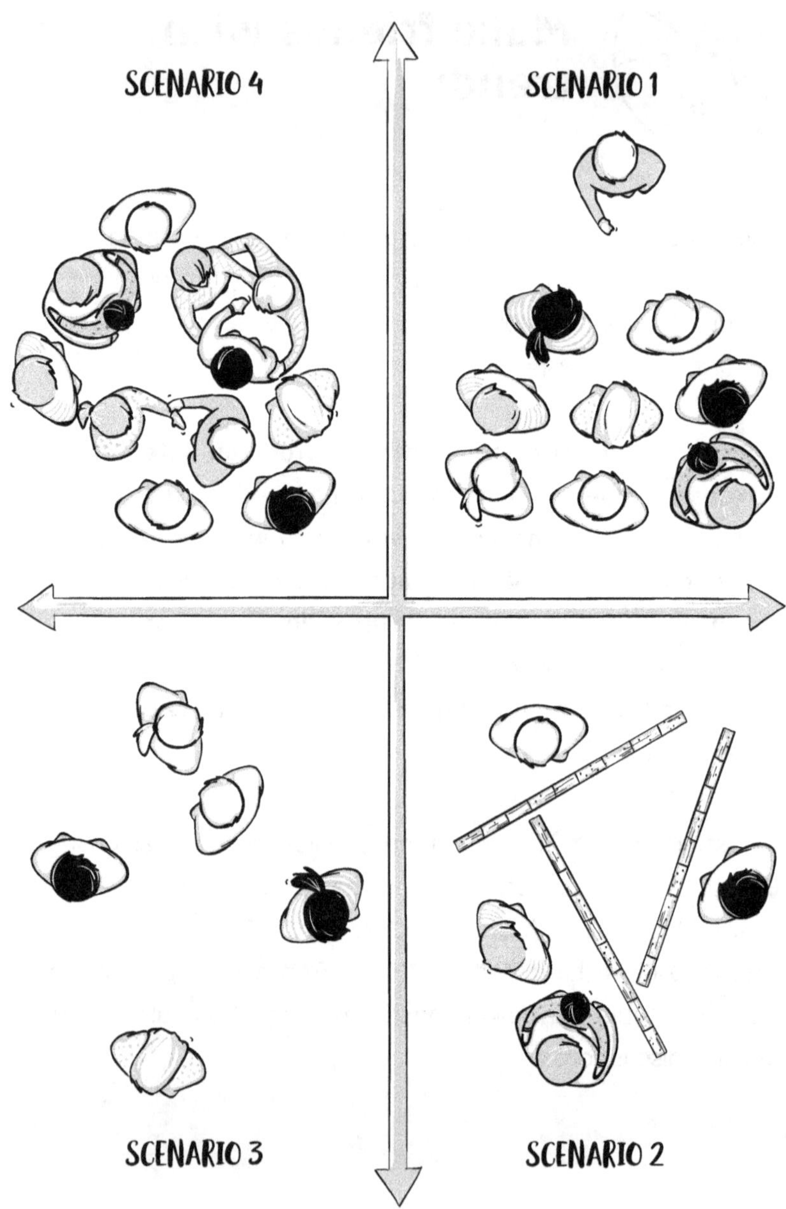

SCENARIO 4
SCENARIO 1
SCENARIO 3
SCENARIO 2

7 Scenarios Open the Mind

Spring 2020. Millions of people around the globe sit at home. They work from home, learn from home, shop from home, and are entertained at home. Thousands of people die, health care systems in many countries are overburdened, politics is overstretched, the economy is shrinking. Why were we not better prepared? Why did nobody see this coming? Did nobody see it coming? Some saw it. On the one hand, the health experts who warned years before about possible pandemics. On the other hand, those who drew up future scenarios and described pandemics in them. For example, in one of four scenarios from the Rockefeller Foundation in 2010, a virus kills eight million people worldwide and brings international trade and tourism to a standstill. Only China reacts quickly and decisively enough in this scenario to contain the virus. The Chinese economy is soon back on its feet. From the perspective of the year 2021, this is an eerie view. Such scenarios cannot be created by analyzing past trends alone. What is needed is a method that opens the mind further: The scenario method.

Open to different futures

The scenario method is now widely used and comes in different variants. One possibility is to describe one scenario that is significantly better than the official forecast of the future and one scenario that is significantly worse. This is a rather limited approach and remains close to extrapolating the past. In this variant, little consideration is given to the openness of the future. This means that there can be no results such as those from a scenario process on the future of private banking, which I facilitated. They were called "ex-GDR" and "the leaf-cutting ant", among others.

I like to use the adaptive scenario method, which was developed in the 1970s by the Shell oil company under the direction of Pierre Wack. He aimed to develop a better way of dealing with the uncertain, open future in addition to trends and forecasts. Legend has it that Shell was better prepared for the unexpected oil price shock after the 1973 Yom Kippur War through its scenario work. At that time, the price of oil quadrupled within a few years. Car-free Sundays and driving bans followed. Peter Schwartz, who followed Pierre Wack as head of scenario planning at Shell in 1982, further refined the method and widely disseminated it in articles and a book.

A question to begin with

Every scenario process starts with a relevant question to which one does not know the answer and cannot know the answer because there are many possible developments on which one has only limited influence. For example: How might technological progress affect the evolution of society 20 years from now? How could the economic situation in China develop over the next ten years? What could my career prospects look like until retirement? There is usually a time horizon associated with every question and every scenario process. It should be sufficiently far ahead to allow for open thinking and at the same time still allow for a connection to current actions.

Then it is necessary to bring into the process those people that could offer helpful input on the guiding question. This includes people with different perspectives, backgrounds, and experiences. Not only the experts, who always talk to each other anyway, but also people with different perspectives. And ideally, people should be involved who can take the results into account in their decision-making. Because here, as everywhere else, if you have been involved in the creation of something yourself, then it is more likely that you will adopt the results.

Value from communication

The mechanics of such an adaptive scenario process is relatively simple. First, many possible factors influencing the topic are collected. Then these factors are sorted according to the importance of their influence and the uncertainty about their future development. Then the two factors that are particularly important and at the same time particularly uncertain are selected. They are used to construct a scenario cross: the two major uncertainties are placed along the two axes, each with high/positive and low/negative characteristics. A coherent picture of the future is then described for each quadrant, which also includes the other influencing factors. The result is four more or less detailed descriptions of the future, which differ significantly from one another.

While the mechanics are not particularly complicated, the major challenges and the great added value arise in the practical implementation of a scenario process. Here it becomes obvious to the participants how many influencing factors can play a role. It also becomes apparent that different people have different assessments of the significance and uncertainty of these influencing factors. Data are collected, trend analyses are prepared. Amid this variety, process facilitators ensure that people do not get bogged down in detailed discussions for months on end but find a way to the next step in the process. Also, descriptions of the future are developed that may be irritating and have little in common with the official future. In my view, all this is the real added value of a scenario process: communication between disciplines, departments, silos, perspectives, or world views is promoted, as is knowledge of the complex interrelationships behind the respective guiding question. This value-added can be more easily accessed when the future suddenly turns out to be different from what was thought and different from each of the four scenarios developed in the process.

The results of this work are not forecasts or probabilities for individual scenarios. The actual development will not correspond exactly to one of them anyway. Probably it will be a rather confusing mixture of several scenarios. However, these can help to make better sense of new information and to initiate appropriate actions. Indicators can be developed that can be used to check whether the system is moving towards a particular scenario as time passes. Options for robust actions can be developed, which are likely to contribute to a reasonably desirable outcome in each of the scenarios and are also easy to adapt. In complex, adaptive, emergent systems this is a coherent approach.

This adaptive scenario method is particularly suitable for topics on whose future development one has little influence, such as the price of oil. One is enabled to think in different futures, to better deal with the openness and uncertainty of the future. One learns to be better prepared for eventualities. If there is room for influence, you can even try to work towards the realization of the most positive scenario.

The transformative scenario method

Adam Kahane, who after Wack and Schwartz had been in charge of scenario work at Shell, was not satisfied with this adaptive perspective. He wanted to actively change the future through transformative scenarios, ideally to improve it. To achieve this, he prefers to work with people who can influence future developments. He became famous for his project after the end of apartheid in South Africa. In 1991, at the "Mont Fleur" conference center outside Cape Town, he moderated a process involving 22 black and white leaders from politics, business, and civil society. He worked with three major uncertainties that built on each other: Would a settlement be negotiated? Would the transition be rapid and decisive? And would the government's policies be sustainable?

The analysis focused on the various options without evaluating them. Kahane's hope was, however, that those present during the process would work together to promote the scenario that everyone considered most desirable and thus make it more likely. It was not the "Ostrich" with the heads of the white minority in the sand, the "Lame Duck" with a coalition government unable to make decisions, nor the "Icarus" of an unsustainable policy. The only scenario that was attractive in the long term was the "Flight of the Flamingos", in which a societal transformation was achieved. The scenarios were illustrated and published in major South African newspapers. After the process, politicians repeatedly made public references to the flamingo scenario, which was thereby anchored in the minds of decision-makers and the population.

Kahane uses transformative scenario planning when three conditions are met: Firstly, the issue at stake is an unstable, unacceptable, unsustainable situation, a fact that is clear to everyone involved. Secondly, the individual actors cannot solve the situation on their own, for example by forcing others in a certain direction. Rather, the cooperation of the whole system is necessary. And thirdly, the problem cannot be tackled directly, because a solution would first have to be agreed upon, which in turn would require strengthening relationships and promoting understanding for each other. Only then does a common goal emerge and action can be directed towards it. In recent years, Kahane has made it less important to agree on a common goal. In many complex situations, such a goal is too ambitious. He is now concentrating on the joint development of new ideas for solutions to concrete challenges. This is in line with the insights gained in futures literacy, where new ideas and questions are developed rather than visions of the future that must be agreed upon by all.

Impact of scenario work

The great challenge for any futures work is the question of whether it makes a difference, improves something. Are better solutions found than without the scenario process? This is difficult to substantiate, especially since the cross-check to the situation without the process is not available and we usually cannot know what is "better". Have new ideas and further questions been developed? This can be determined with reasonable reliability. Have new relationships and new trust been established that provide a better basis for future cooperation? This can be observed through surveys before, directly after, and several months after a process. Has the information base been improved and made visible? Well-designed publications and their dissemination are helpful in this respect, which is relatively easy to observe.

Many possibilities
for many scenarios

There are different ways for you to use the insights of this chapter: You can embark on a systematic and ideally collaborative search for important uncertainties on your topic. What are important factors influencing the future of your organization or your industry where you honestly cannot know where they will go? Make these uncertainties visible, discuss them with your colleagues - perhaps even with the help of the scenario method.

You could also read the books by Peter Schwartz "The Art of the Long View - Planning for the Future in an Uncertain World" (1991), by Kees van der Heijden "Scenarios - The Art of Strategic Conversation" (1996/2005), or by Adam Kahane "Transformative Scenario Planning - Working Together to Change the Future" (2013).

8 Visions: Images of Desirable Futures

Many people have a more or less clear idea of what their future should look like, what they see for themselves there. They have a vision (Latin: visio). Or they may even have several pictures of different successful futures. And probably also pictures of how their future should not look like. These ideas are all too human. Even more: Our ideas of the future are the only thing we can know about the future today. After all, we cannot go there to explore and measure it.

While trends and scenarios try to look at probable and possible futures, visions are the gateway to what we want and what is somewhat realistic. In contrast, utopias are supposedly unrealistic places in the future. And dystopias are images of what we would like to avoid.

An important building block

Visions are an important building block in many larger futures processes: In Future Search (chapter 10), the vision consists of the lowest common denominator of the various stakeholders of the topic. In Futures Literacy Laboratories (chapter 12), discussions about desirable futures make the assumptions of those involved visible and create the basis for experiments with alternative futures. In Appreciative Inquiry (chapter 13) they are the dream that builds on the positive experiences of the present. In quality-of-life processes (chapters 17 to 19) they are the summary of the dialogue phase and the basis for the search for suitable indicators.

Visions always bring with them a danger or challenge: they are only the summary of a single possible future and can obscure the view of alternative futures. While a vision is being developed, divergent views have little room. They are put aside as minority opinions or somehow reformulated to fit. And when a vision is agreed upon, it shapes the perception of those involved. This is exactly the purpose of visions. However, by this fixation on a single future, other possible developments could be overlooked or ignored. This danger can be reduced in longer-term visioning processes by working with scenarios or alternative futures as well.

Another limit of scenarios is the way they deal with emergence. Visions arise from the values and preferences of the past and the present. On this basis, how can we recognize whether something new is desirable or not? It would be so important to know whether we want to strengthen the newly created or get rid of it quickly. The solution seems to be to formulate visions in sufficiently general terms so that new things can be assessed against them. If, for example, freedom, variety, and openness are recurring elements of visions of the future, then every new legislative project, every product innovation, and every start-up should be measured by them.

Visions often consist of great hopes. And great hopes are placed in them. Ideally, they motivate people to commit themselves individually or collectively to this future and to invest resources in its implementation. If one has the impression that others are working with their possibilities for a greater common cause, then one is more willing to do so as well. Ideally, therefore, visions have a clear connection to action in the present.

Requirements for visions

With visions, the wishes of many participants are united in a mosaic-like manner to form an overall picture. That sounds easier than it is. In practice, several requirements should be met:

▎ First, visions should be formulated positively. They bring together what we want more of, what we want to strengthen. In this way, a positive basic attitude is adopted, which sends signals of confidence and - hopefully not too unrealistic - the potential for improvement. Thus, the problems and weaknesses that are to be solved or reduced are not listed. There is no struggling against undesirable conditions, which is usually not very enjoyable and often requires a lot of energy. The point here is not to close one's eyes to the problems, but to formulate them positively in the vision. For example, the 2019 petition for a referendum in the German state of Bavaria was partly successful because it was not against pesticides or over-fertilization but was supportive of biodiversity and natural beauty.

❚ Secondly, visions should be shared collectively if they are to be accepted and supported by the target group. Only then will people in a free society stand up for their implementation. Only then can the vision release additional energy as a link between people. In theory, such a broadly accepted vision can also be developed by a small group of smart, forward-thinking people. In time, other people will understand why that vision is so good for them. In a business context, this may be a practically relevant option. Think of the charisma and vision of Steve Jobs at Apple. On the societal level, however, participatory visions seem to be more promising. That may be because you are more likely to accept results if you have been involved in their creation. Or it may be because of the greater collective intelligence that brings more different perspectives together. With the help of competent process facilitation, it is possible to deal constructively with these different value concepts.

❚ Visions should, thirdly, be clearly presented so that they can be easily understood by everyone in the target group. Besides text in easy language, pictures, drawings, videos, graphics, and other means can be used to make the desirable futures visible. In discussions with illustrators or writers, other important aspects of the future can also be uncovered or clarified.

■ The fourth requirement for powerful visions is the challenge or ambition that goes with them. If the vision of the future is already largely a reality today or is automatically achieved without any effort on one's part, then no common energy can be released for its implementation.

■ Fifthly, visions should be adaptable and should not become dogmas. If the environment changes over time, if new issues prove to be important, if people's values change, then the vision should also be adapted. In larger visioning processes a revision should be possible every four or five years: Is what we collected back then still important to us? What developments have there been since then?

It is also necessary that the time horizon and target group for the vision are clear. The next year is usually too short a time horizon, the year 2100 unimaginably far away for many. Most visions, therefore, refer to a time horizon between 5 and 30 years. Target groups can be the employees of a company, all inhabitants of a city, a country, or the whole world. Or individual groups, such as children, nursing staff, or journalists.

Finally, it seems fundamentally helpful if the vision process is anchored at one or more relevant institutions. These can be the nodal point where the various threads of vision creation come together, provide visibility, and accompany implementation. These institutions should be neutral in terms of content, i.e. do not influence the results in their interest. For example, party-political actors are rarely seen as neutral, since the respective opposition is fundamentally skeptical about the results.

A shared image of the future

Visions do not necessarily have to be innovative and surprising. Some seem rather boring and familiar at first glance. That is a good thing. Because then it is likely that a collectively shared vision of the future has indeed been revealed. The value of a vision does not lie in the controversy, but in the common ground. An example:

"[...] is an economically prosperous society in which people live together peacefully and do not place too much strain on the natural environment. People enjoy good health, a high level of education, meaningful work, a wide range of cultural opportunities, and contribute to community decision-making. "

Here, most people would nod in agreement, which is a good basis for action to achieve this future. A low innovation potential does not mean that one could simply adopt the vision of the neighboring country or city. Even if the result would be largely congruent, nuances can be decisive, and above all the feeling of having contributed to drafting this vision. What is important is the comparison with the current situation and the willingness to commit oneself to the vision.

Joy in positive futures

Vision work is possible in many places at all levels. In a company, a school, or in a city. What is decisive is the dialogue about what is important to people, what kind of future they want. Why do we do this, what drives us, what values should our vision contain?

Start such a process in your field. Develop a good question, think about who should participate in the discussion, and facilitate a dialogue about it. Start small. Find comrades-in-arms, avoid opponents. Enjoy working together towards positive futures.

 Where We Are: Indicators

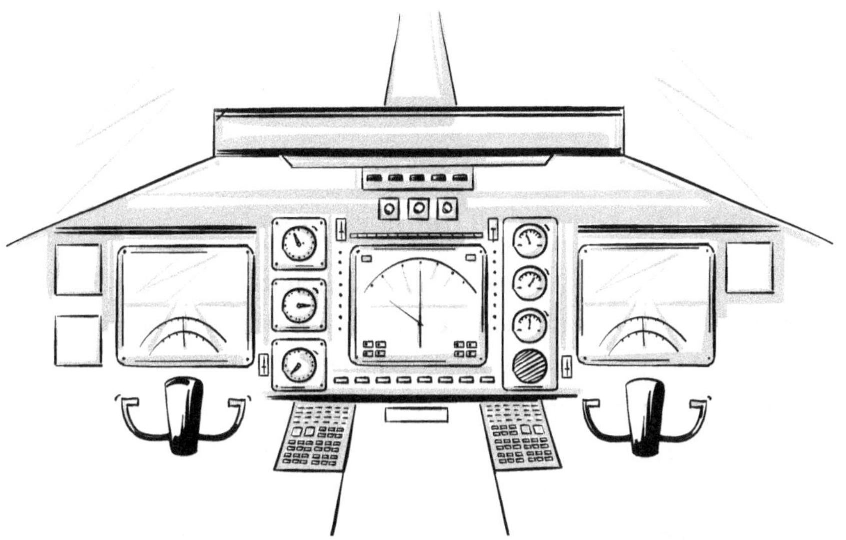

"You know that I don't believe in it. But go ahead anyway." That was the reaction of my then supervisor, the chief economist of Deutsche Bank, Norbert Walter, when I told him in 2005 about my plans to study broad measures of societal progress. In a report, I wanted to include survey data, i.e. subjective indicators of quality of life and life satisfaction. This was and still is unfamiliar territory for many economists. All the more reason for me to be grateful to Norbert Walter for letting me do it. He later even created the title of the German report "BIP allein macht nicht glücklich" (GDP alone does not make you happy), in keeping with the popular saying that "Geld allein macht nicht glücklich" (money alone does not make you happy).

The report caused quite a stir inside and outside the bank. Not all economists in the bank at the time recognized the importance of broad welfare measurement. Outside the bank, some interpreted the report as a marketing campaign to improve the bank's image. They underestimated the independence of the researchers in the bank. Others used the report to promote their topics: "Even Deutsche Bank says…" They underestimated the importance of researchers in the bank.

Numbers are needed in many places

Without reliable and relevant indicators, futures research would depend only on opinions about the current situation. An indicator (Lat. indicare) should show whether a certain state is present. Body temperature is an important indicator of a person's health. Over the centuries, ways have been found to measure body temperature with increasing accuracy and it has been found that values above 38 degrees indicate illness. However, we also know that a temperature of 37 degrees does not rule out illness. To find a suitable therapy, one usually needs additional indicators such as the heart rate, blood pressure, or pain sensation.

If you follow these indicators over time, you can see the success or failure of the therapy: If the fever drops, the patient appears to be on the road to recovery and the medication is working. The same applies to complex societal systems. To find out how a country or city is doing, people's income is an important indicator. But income alone cannot provide an overall picture. We need other relevant indicators. And ideally, we need to track their development over time so that we can determine whether something is improving or deteriorating.

In futures research, data and indicators provide important support and insights in many areas. This is particularly obvious for trend analysis. It is based on data that experts interpret as indicators of certain developments. The experts make the selection from their perspectives. In a scenario process, indicators are jointly decided on in the course of the work: With their help, it should be possible to check whether the system is developing in the direction of one scenario.

Sometimes the appropriate indicators are already available. Sometimes they are only decided in the process. Then ways are sought to collect them or to obtain them from specialists. For example: At what height above sea level and at what points in time should the concentration of CFCs be measured by which organization to be able to map the size of the ozone hole? Often new, relevant indicators require additional time and financial effort. And often compromises are made because the perfect indicators cannot be found. At the same time, the discussion about indicators can help to further clarify the issues.

In visioning processes, indicators help above all to identify the need for action: Once the visions have been formulated, suitable indicators are compiled to cover the entire range of topics. On this basis, we can find out where there is a big gap between the actual and the desired situation. White spots in the database are ideally eliminated by accessing new sources or by conducting new surveys. In a visioning process, a dozen different sources may be needed plus some placeholders for data not yet available. When it comes to relatively new topics such as digitalization, you quickly realize how little robust data you have on important issues. Do we know, for example, whether digital technologies are more likely to promote people's self-determination or promote external control? Do they contribute more to adaptation or to variety? Representative population surveys can provide a first, subjective impression. If we do not have anything better at the moment, we should go this way - always aware of the limitations.

Futures and quality-of-life research

The connection between futures research and quality-of-life research is obvious. Often enough, futures research is about "Creating Better Futures" (the title of the book by James Ogilvy), which scenarios are desirable or, more generally, what world we want to live in. In most futures processes, normative questions about a good, successful life come up. This is precisely what quality-of-life research is all about, which develops appropriate indicators and often also interventions that are intended to improve that quality of life. It is about measuring what is important and measurable.

In addition to being related to the scenarios or visions that have been jointly developed, indicators should meet several other requirements to be helpful:

▐ First, they should be outcome-oriented. In the case of a sick person, we measure his or her wellbeing by body temperature rather than by the amount of medicine taken. Similarly, the educational success of a society should not be measured by the expenditure on it. Expenditure can go to waste without effect. On the other hand, positive effects can also be achieved without financial expenditure. It is better to measure the acquired skills - if these can be depicted reasonably well with data.

Secondly, each indicator should be accompanied by a clear assessment of its direction. In visioning processes, the question arises as to the desired development of the indicator. In scenario processes, the question is which scenario is consistent with a decline or an increase of the indicator. The preferred direction of indicators is not always clear. For example, the proportion of people in the population who are older than 65 years can be interpreted in several directions. For some, a higher proportion expresses a desirable trend towards a longer life expectancy. Others see an increase as a burden on pension systems and a decline in innovative strength. Here, more appropriate indicators need to be sought, such as life expectancy itself or the relative proportions of pensioners and contributors, presumably with a desire for stability of the ratio.

Thirdly, the values of the indicators should be changeable by human intervention - like the body temperature of sick people. Then the appropriate actions can be initiated, i.e. taking medication or giving special support to children from disadvantaged backgrounds. This change should lead to a real improvement and not just be cosmetic. If, for example, many unemployed people are removed from the statistics by a change in definition, the official data look better, but there has not been a real improvement. Or if the number of school leavers without a lower secondary degree is reduced by particularly easy exams, then education has not improved. These are examples of Charles Goodhardt's famous rule according to which indicators become useless as soon as they become political objectives and values are managed accordingly.

Fourthly, the indicators should be easy to understand. Body temperature is familiar and understandable to us all. Most people have heard so much about Gross Domestic Product (GDP) that they think it is a measure of economic activity and accept it without knowing exactly how it is calculated. If one points out the special features of the calculation, then parallel to the increasing understanding, doubts are also raised about the significance of GDP for prosperity. A technically well-designed indicator of educational mobility between parents and children may be highly relevant, but it is probably understandable only to a few experts.

▌ Fifth, one can try to combine objective and subjective indicators wisely. An objective measure of security in a city is the number of reported crimes. However, this number can be influenced by the intensity of police work or the tendency to report a crime. Add to this people's subjective feeling of security ("Do you feel safe in your city at night?") and a clearer overall picture emerges. A low feeling of security combined with a low crime rate leads to different conclusions than a high crime rate.

▌ Sixth, it would be important and desirable for the indicators to be available on time and as time series. Values that refer to a point in time three years ago are hardly useful in the early warning system of a scenario process. A single data point cannot give us any information about an improvement or deterioration over time. Some indicators are now available in real-time (outdoor temperature), others daily (Covid-19 infected people), others monthly (unemployment data), quarterly (gross domestic product), or annually (life expectancy of people). Some of these indicators are immediately available, while others take a few days or weeks to calculate. All of this must be considered when selecting the indicators to be used in a futures process.

Indicators to understand the present

Do not be put off by the high demands on good indicators but try to use numbers to better understand the present. Do not be afraid of their shortcomings and the many pitfalls. Make those visible and discuss the challenges on the way.

> **Look for better indicators that reflect more of what you really want to measure. Are you dissatisfied with high-school graduation rates or PISA results as measures of a good education because you are interested in education for people's self-empowerment? How about asking people about their control over their own lives ("locus of control")? This indicator already exists. Whatever you want to measure, go and find the best data available.**

If you would like to read reports with many indicators on quality of life: My report on "The Happy Variety of Capitalism 2.0" is freely available electronically in English as are the results from the quality-of-life processes "Wellbeing in Germany" (see also chapter 18) and "Quality of Life in the Digital Age" (#gutlebendigital, chapter 19). Or take a look at Hans Rosling's book "Factfulness - Ten Reasons We're Wrong About The World - And Why Things Are Better".

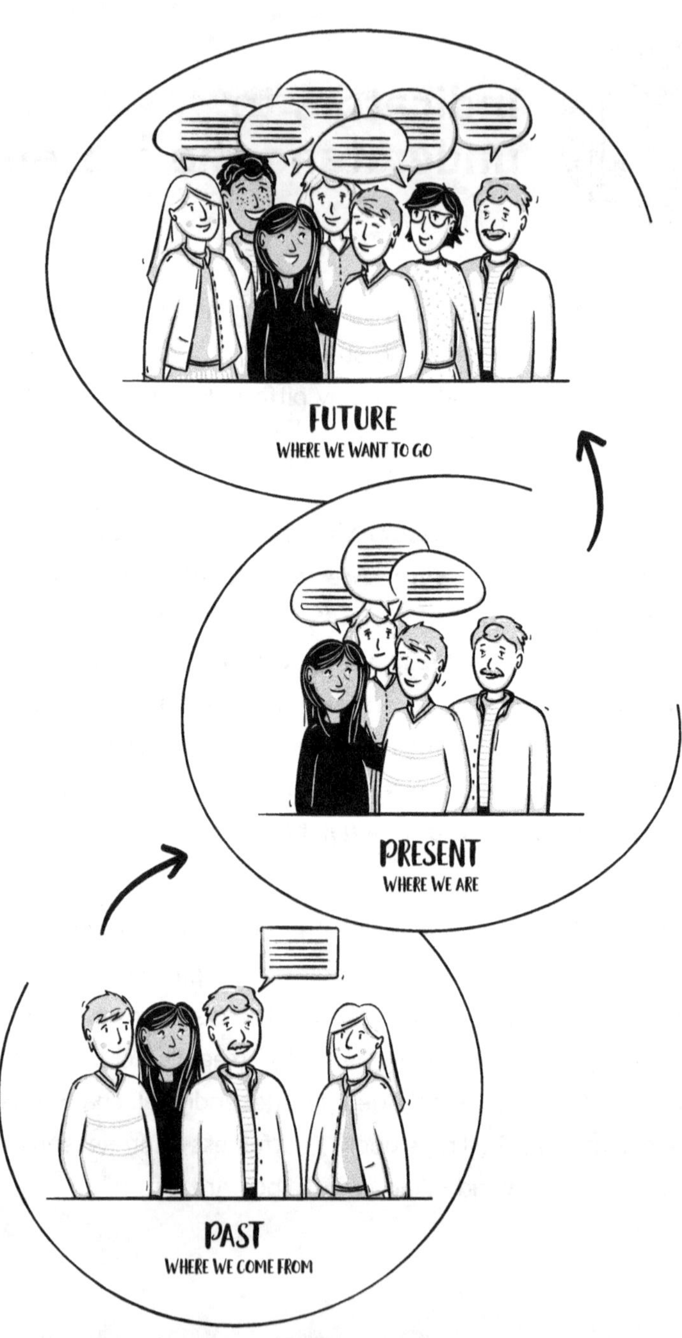

FUTURE
WHERE WE WANT TO GO
PRESENT
WHERE WE ARE
PAST
WHERE WE COME FROM

10 Searching for a Common Future

Late on a Friday evening in the rooms of a foundation in central Berlin in 2013. The heads of twenty younger executives from politics, business, science, media, and culture are spinning. A lot of men are in the room, most of them close to the conservative party CDU. Since the early afternoon, I have been working with them on the topic "Germany in 2040". Now everyone involved is surprised: "social peace" became visible as the most important common base for a desirable future. Not "high economic growth", "strong exports" or "low taxes", as I and probably others in the room may have suspected at the beginning of the meeting. But social peace. Life satisfaction, individuality, openness, and sustainability also met broad approval. In the course of the day, we had brought together the perspectives of the participants, used the collective intelligence in the room to make visible an important topic that would increasingly occupy many countries in the years to come: social peace.

As a process facilitator, I used the method of "Future Search" on this day in a small, shortened version. This method is helpful when different stakeholder groups come together on a rather controversial topic and want to search for common ground for their activities. Alternating between small groups and the plenary, we discussed the highlights of the past, collected the trends of the present, and formulated wishes for the future.

The collective intelligence of all involved

Future Search was developed by Marvin Weisbord and Sandra Janoff and has been used around the globe for decades. I see it as a particularly helpful approach to working with complex societal systems. It relies not only on individual experts but on the collective intelligence of all those involved. It is less about solving specific problems (which often corresponds to the treatment of symptoms), but rather about their causes in the entire system.

The process that Weisbord and Janoff developed is both strict and demanding. From my point of view, this is the ideal setting from which one can select individual elements to suit the specific conditions. The following description of the method should on the one hand show how well thought through it is. On the other hand, it should also make you want to try out individual elements on a small scale.

In Future Search, representatives of the entire system should come together in one room. If, for example, the future of education is being discussed, ideally students, parents, teachers, administration, politicians, companies, and scientists should be present. Weisbord and Janoff prefer to work with eight groups with eight members each for a total of 64 participants. Anyone who has ever attended or even moderated an event with just two or three of the mentioned groups knows how ambitious this requirement is. The challenges for the invitation process and for the design of the event are considerable. The important point is that you should try to involve as many groups as possible.

The requirement becomes even higher if these 64 people ideally meet for two days from noon on the first day to noon on the third day. This is a major commitment of time, which should be accompanied by a high expectation of effectiveness. One will not always live up to this ideal. In the example "Germany in 2040" we did not have the whole system in the room, but more elements than many other, rather homogeneous events. And we only had an afternoon and an evening at our disposal. But it was a fine way to achieve results that go beyond what is possible at classic lecture events and panel discussions.

Past, present, and future

After an introduction to the objectives and the course of the event, all participants first introduce themselves. Ideally, this is done in mixed teams with one person from each of the different societal groups. And it happens on a personal level, for example by exchanging formative experiences in one's own life. In this way first connections are made between the groups and the professional level of interest is initially pushed into the background. This is an important starting point that can be applied at any event, so that later on participants can work together constructively across individual interests.

The next step is to look at the past. First, all participants write down the major events or milestones in society and on the respective topic. They position them on timelines on the wall. Then the mixed groups use them to create stories that bring these insights together. These stories are presented in the plenary and then discussed again in the mixed teams. In this way, it is possible to see the different emphases one brings from the past. Differences in language and terminology are revealed, which in turn is an important prerequisite for sustainable collaboration in the next steps.

From the past participants come to the present and to the trends that influence the topic today. All participants write down the most important trends by themselves. Then they all together work on a structured overview. The aim here is to obtain an overall view of the most important developments in social, technological, economic, ecological, cultural, and political issues. In this way, white spots can become visible and topics with high attention. Both are helpful in any futures process. The different groups can then discuss two or three trends in-depth: For example, what impact do these trends have on a specific group? How are they related to other trends? How do we deal with the trends today? What could we do with them in the future?

For the harvest in the plenary, they then collect the current actions of this group, of which they are particularly proud concerning the theme of the event. And their actions that they may regret or that they would approach differently in retrospect. They could say: "As parents, we are sorry that we did not pay more attention to the trend of increasing digitalization." The presentation in the plenary and the subsequent discussion will promote understanding of the topic and the situation of the different societal groups.

Once this foundation has been laid, and the understanding of the language and the perspectives of the other groups has been strengthened, the future can come into play. In the mixed teams from the beginning of the event, desired futures of the topic in the chosen time horizon are developed. Visions. What do we want to see in the future? Which programs and structures exist? Which interactions? What was done by whom to get there? As the groups present their visions of the future, all participants write down the elements that seem to be important to everyone in the room. These elements are then first discussed and sorted in the homogeneous groups. What is important to all members of this group and probably also to the members of the other groups?

Searching for common ground

Then these elements are collected in plenary, controversial points are set aside. The resulting collections of similar points can then be deepened in small groups: What exactly does this aspect of a future desired by all participants look like? The groups then present their results in the plenary. Finally, the planning of the actions starts: Which group can do what to make this jointly worked out desirable future more likely? What contribution will each individual make?

Future Search is an important method for making visible the variety of perspectives on a topic. It is not about quarreling and arguing, nor is it about everyone agreeing on everything. Differences are made visible. However, the focus is on the search for common ground. In this way, a clear basis for future action is laid. Participants see the connection between what they want to do themselves and what others do. Everybody contributes to a whole. A Future Search can dissolve paralysis, generate new ideas, give hope, make connections, strengthen community, and is thus an important contribution to shaping the future. There are enough topics that call for such an approach: The future of health, mobility, education, or work.

No futures method can offer everything. The focus of Future Search is on common ground and on planning for the future. There is the danger of being fixated on one, narrow vision of the future. Large uncertainties such as those highlighted in a scenario process lie outside the focus. Therefore, the method should be used above all when one has a great influence on the future of this topic, if planning is possible. Also, Future Search does not pursue controversial topics much further. Time bombs may be slumbering here, which may explode later and destroy what participants achieved together. On the other hand, they could also be seeds of truly new and creative solutions that would later allow a completely different view of the future. Seed bombs perhaps, for which there is no common ground today simply because they are too new, too little visible.

Needed: Hosts with a high reputation

The most important prerequisite for a Future Search is that the various groups agree to join in this type of collaboration. Similar to what is required for a transformative scenario process, they have realized that the other possibilities do not lead to long-term desirable situations: The powerful ones realize that the exercise of power by a single group is neither social nor democratic - and is often accompanied by negative side effects. The passive ones are motivated to get involved. And the external critics engage in dialogue with the other actors. Also, neutral hosts with a high reputation are needed, who have the necessary financial and methodological resources to make such a process possible.

In the example of "Germany in 2040", 20 senior leaders from different sectors had come together and got involved in this type of work. Unfortunately, the originally planned follow-up event on the next steps and concrete actions did not take place. I am not sure why: Were people shocked by the unexpected core result of "social peace"? Did they realize that the next step would have to be a meeting with other social groups on this topic? Were they concerned that possible recommendations for action would trigger unpleasant controversies in their communities? Or were they simply completely occupied with "day-to-day business"? Who knows, perhaps some of the unpleasant developments of recent years such as the rise of extremist political parties could have been slowed down if we had devoted ourselves more intensively to the topic of "social peace" together.

Invitation to other groups

Running a two-day Future Search with 64 participants will probably only be possible for few of us. But there are many possibilities to use individual elements of this method.

> **For example, you can provide a space to make visible past successes on an important topic. And you can invite other groups who are working on the same topic appreciatively and openly. Perhaps starting with an innocuous discussion about the major trends of the present. Within your organization, you can facilitate more dialogue and clarity about shared elements of a desirable future.**

The original book "Future Search - Getting the Whole System in the Room for Vision, Commitment and Action" by Marvin Weisbord and Sandra Janoff is recommended for reading.

 11 Looking at Several Levels

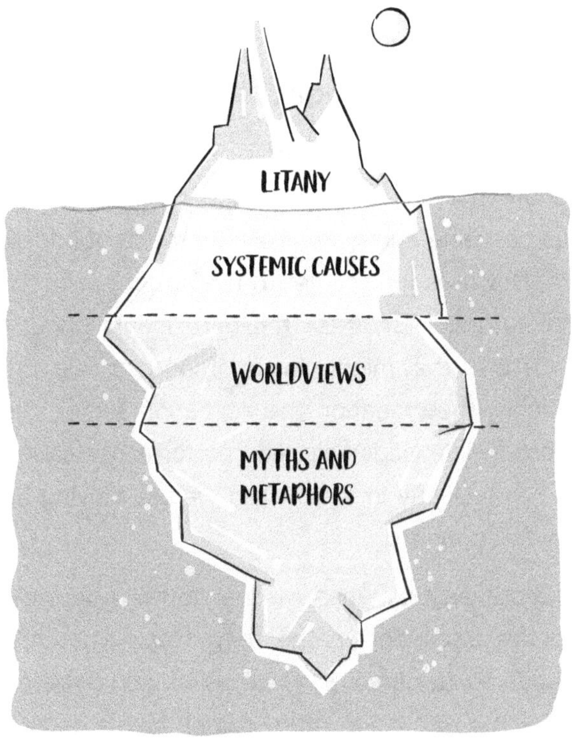

May 2019 on the well-cooled 52nd floor of the Emirates Tower in Dubai. Here, at the seat of the government of the United Arab Emirates, I am using a relatively new method for examining futures, the Causal Layered Analysis. On behalf of UNESCO, we are preparing two major events for the autumn and are now testing some possible elements together with government representatives. We are talking about the futures of the public sector and the futures of education in the Emirates in 2050. Having already discussed probable and desirable futures, trends, and visions, we are now drilling deeper. We work in different layers: the visible litany, the underlying systemic causes, the worldviews, and finally the myths and metaphors.

Develop alternative images

A slim and virtual public sector that is oriented towards the needs of the population and works closely together across departments had emerged as desirable and quite likely. So far so good, so useful, so well-known. Now it is time to get to the bottom of this widespread view of the future. First, I ask the participants about the actors and the structures that might play an important role in this future. Not surprisingly, they mention the education sector, technological progress, responsible leadership, and performance orientation. This showed us more clearly in which field we are moving and who we need to pay attention to.

Things get more exciting when we turn to the worldviews of those involved in the discussion in the third step: What attitudes and values are behind the litany? Which assumptions become visible? This is where the discussion often comes to a standstill, as these are unusual questions in many places. We grope our way to values such as equality, freedom, flexibility, or competition. The big issues and topics. There is no longer any talk of digitalization, air taxis, or artificial intelligence. Those stay in the background as part of the litany that opened the way to the discussion of values.

In the fourth step, I ask my group to summarize in a slogan what their future is all about. What image, what metaphor would they use? "We create a dynamic future" was the coherent and extremely valuable result. At first, there was even talk of "We control the future", which the group felt was too lofty. With this deep understanding of the litany, actors, worldviews, and the metaphor behind it, it was now time to open the horizon further and talk about alternatives. Is there another metaphor that might draw attention to other worldviews and other actors? This is a difficult task in any context, in any government, and any larger organization. In this specific group, we came up with the "horizontal flow of power" as an alternative image. This image might lead to different organizational, political, and technological expressions, not only in the public sector, compared to our discussions at the beginning of the exercise. This was a fascinating turn of events, made possible by the method chosen.

Question, interpret, act

The method I was able to apply in Dubai is the "Causal Layered Analysis" or CLA for short. It was developed in the 1990s by the Pakistani futurist Sohail Inayatullah based on his studies at the University of Hawaii. This makes it one of the more recent methods and one that did not initially reflect the needs of the American military. Before this, the Delphi method and the scenario method were initially developed in the 1950s by the RAND Corporation (Research AND Development), which was founded after the end of the Second World War to advise the US military during the Cold War.

As a student at the University of Hawaii, Inayatullah became aware of the tensions between different approaches within the politics department, which he found unfruitful: The empiricists placed particular emphasis on facts and data. They wanted to analyze politics as scientifically as possible. On the other hand, the representatives of critical theory questioned everything: the object of investigation, the research question, or the power structures behind it. In between, he saw the interpretive approach, which aims at conversations, shared meaning, and significance. Action research was also present, in which researchers and those affected work closely together. Inayatullah wondered why these approaches were not linked. Step by step, he established these links. The Causal Layered Analysis emerged. He was also influenced by the work of the Norwegian conflict researcher Johan Galtung, the French philosopher Michel Foucault, the Indian philosopher Prabhat Ranjan Sarkar and complexity research.

In my 2009 report "Zukunftsforschung für Staaten" (Futures Studies for States) I had prepared a summary of the method in German. Within the ten methods I presented at the time, I classified it as particularly demanding and elaborate, and at the same time as a particularly suitable approach for complex, long-term issues.

In my processes since then, I have consciously or unconsciously tried to combine as many CLA-levels as possible and to drill as deep as possible. As a trained empiricist, I still consider data and indicators important. These are always interpreted and ideally a connection is made to dialogue and commonly shared ideas about desirable futures. This can only succeed together with those affected. Along the way, there should be room to ask critical questions without burying the whole project and without being unable to act. My preferred sequence is dialogue, visions, indicators, actions - which should always be linked to each other.

The method of Causal Layered Analysis has a clear structure:

Level 1: The litany. Here, quantitative trends and facts are discussed for the topic under investigation, problems are described, events are noted and headlines in the press are discussed. Everything visible on the surface is collected. This requires relatively few analytical skills on the part of the participants and little experience of the process facilitators. It feels easy. The problem is there, it seems to be clearly defined. At the same time, there seem to be hardly any possible solutions, or one refers to "politics" or "business" for solving it. Proposed solutions only deal with the symptoms that have become visible here. If this is too superficial for participants, they are ready for the second level.

Level 2: The system. Now the question is asked which cultural, historical, economic, and political factors caused the problem described. The focus of attention turns to the various actors and their decisions. Data, facts, and observations from the litany are connected and interpreted. Causes and effects are described. This requires professional expertise and process facilitation that maintains an overview of all the connections. Proposed solutions usually focus on joint action by several actors to fundamentally change the system. More profound questions are not yet asked at this level. Together with the litany from level 1, the foundation for the next level is laid.

Level 3: The worldviews. Now the deeper social, linguistic, and cultural patterns that affect all actors are explored. The assumptions behind the structures are made visible and alternative assumptions are examined. The different discourses on the topic and their relative roles are made visible: economic, political, or religious. They represent the framework in which the system and the litany were created. This is unfamiliar terrain for most participants, as it is not usually illuminated in the evening news. Participants are invited to engage with new questions and insights. The process facilitators need a lot of tact and sensitivity to ask the appropriate questions that do not overstrain.

Level 4: The metaphor. After the analysis of the worldviews, the fourth level deals with the emotions that determine the topic at hand, and which were neglected in the other levels. One deals with images, myths, and metaphors that touch the heart rather than the mind. Now you get to the bottom of the topic. Often it is about identities, control, nature, time, life, or death. Does God roll the dice? Are we the makers of our happiness? Is the future a series of conscious decisions, or more a torrential river, or a tree with roots and many shoots? And how does our view of the subject change if we take another metaphor as a basis and use it to work our way back up to the other levels?

This futures method can be applied to various topics. One example that Sohail Inayatullah quotes is the topic of "population explosion". In the litany, population projections are discussed and all the problems caused by more people on the planet. The systems analysis then looks for the reasons for the problem and the connections. What is the role of technological progress, the possible lack of social security, the level of education, what contraceptives are available? What solutions have been proposed by whom and where have they been tried?

The third level then deals with the different worldviews on the issue: what role do women play in the family and society? What interests does business have? Do we need many young people as soldiers against a threatening neighboring state? Or is it biblically about being fruitful and multiplying? All this should be made visible. Only then, in the next step, can one become aware of the deep societal myths or the metaphors that lie behind them. And one can pursue another metaphor. Maybe many people are not a problem, but a source of creativity for the future? What worldviews would support this metaphor, what system would be necessary for it, what headlines would there be?

The Causal Layered Analysis can be combined with other futures methods. Different scenarios can be developed from different metaphors. A desirable future, a vision, can be selected and worked on in-depth. Or a completely different, irritating narrative can be brought in from the outside, inspiring even deeper reflection.

Dig one level deeper

Presumably, you will not be facilitating or participating in a complete causal layered analysis yourself next week.

But you can work with the structure of Inayatullah on many occasions. You can recognize data and headlines as the superficially visible parts of larger contexts. No matter what the topic is. You can ask about the structures and the actors behind them. You can then investigate your worldviews on the topic and those of others. Finally, you can try to trace the deeply rooted myths and metaphors and possible alternatives to them. In short, you could think and work in different futures.

There are many articles by Sohail Inayatullah in which he explains Causal Layered Analysis and illustrates it with many examples. For example, from 2004 his "Causal Layered Analysis: Theory, historical context, and case studies" in his reader, or from 2008 "Six pillars: futures thinking for transformation" in the journal Foresight. He also offers an online course "Become a Futurist" along the six pillars.

12 News from the Futures Literacy Laboratory

March 2009 in the House of Literature in Frankfurt am Main in Germany. We celebrate the opening of the think tank "Center for Societal Progress". One of the speakers has traveled from Paris: Riel Miller, a futurist who has been working for decades around the globe with a wide variety of methods for large organizations and states. He knows the worldwide network of futurists extremely well and has published in several scientific journals. In his presentation, the Canadian native points out that even the best planning cannot cope with the complexity of our societies. Instead, it is necessary to anticipate developments and critically question traditional solution routines to open fresh perspectives for action. In short, the collective capacity to anticipate future developments must be increased.

At that time, after some years at the OECD, the Organization for Economic Cooperation and Development, Riel Miller was active as an independent futurist. Three years later he was appointed head of foresight at UNESCO, the United Nations Educational, Scientific and Cultural Organization, well known for its World Heritage activities. There he began - again globally and multidisciplinary networked - to further develop the theory and practice of Futures Literacy, i.e. the ability to deal competently with the various approaches to the future. On this path, I was able to accompany him on several occasions and to contribute in several places to the book "Transforming the Future - Anticipation in the 21st Century". The framework of analysis presented there also serves as a guide for this book.

Make assumptions visible

The most important tool for investigating and strengthening Futures Literacy is the Futures Literacy Laboratory. It is at the same time a place of training, where Futures Literacy is strengthened, and a research institution, where important insights into the future are made visible. Futures Literacy Labs are always designed to suit the respective topic, the participants, and the available resources. They often follow a four-phase process: Reveal, Reframe, Rethink, Next Steps.

In the first phase, easily accessible assumptions of the participants about the future of the topic at hand are revealed and made visible.

In the laboratory, participants are first invited to imagine the probable future situation of the respective topic. For example, what will the media and journalism look like in 2040? First, the participants write down what they expect, what they see, and experience from the perspective of the year 2040. Then these elements are discussed, sorted, and deepened in small groups. What is particularly visible? Where are perhaps blind spots? Finally, the groups present their views of the probable futures to the other groups.

In the discussions, important prerequisites for a higher competency in dealing with the future are made tangible. Often the participants realize how difficult it is to make a forecast. They become aware of the uncertainty and the complex interrelationships in the topic. Sometimes it becomes clear already here how difficult it is to distinguish between a probable and a desirable future. Do I consider this future development probable because I would like it to happen? Or do I have solid evidence that it will happen? Which trend do I extrapolate? As a rule, the participants also see how strongly their ideas about the future are shaped by man-made narratives, routines, and conventions - or even by Hollywood movies. In this way, they reveal their assumptions about the future and get a first impression that there can be different assumptions, different probable futures. Not all these points are always explored in detail. In this first phase, the main aim is to provide an easy introduction to the topic and to build trust among the participants.

After the probable future developments, attention turns to the desirable futures. Again, from the perspective of a later point in time, again initially in individual work, so that all ideas in the room have a chance of becoming visible, and only later in the plenary. At this point, a deepening with a Causal Layered Analysis, as described in the previous chapter, is often used. The participants are first invited to name headlines, behavior, and objects from the desirable future, the litany. The group discussion then shows whether a future situation becomes visible that is equally desirable for all participants or whether contradictory values, preferences, and assumptions come to light. From there, one can work towards the systemic causes, worldviews, and metaphors of this future. As a result, further anticipatory assumptions become visible. The understanding of the topic and of the other participants is strengthened further.

Making probable and desirable futures visible is also part of other important futures methods such as trend analysis, visioning, or Future Search. This is important, helpful and already brings many new insights. In Futures Literacy Laboratories this is only the first of four phases.

Experiment with a different frame

The next phase reframes the discussion of the topic. It considers the great openness of the future and invites the participants to think even more openly. In this second phase, the participants are invited into a future that is neither likely nor unlikely nor desirable or undesirable. It is different, unusual, irritating. This experiment is intended to stimulate creativity, expand the scope of possibilities, strengthen the imagination and enable innovation. The different frame allows a different view of the topic. Alternatively, one can think of a camera with different filters: depending on which filter is in front of the lens, the picture looks different.

There are several ways to construct this alternative future. Lab designers and facilitators can develop an alternative future in advance that the participants would probably not imagine themselves. For example, it can describe a murmuration society in which many small actors are in flexible exchange with each other, without central control. Or it could develop a strong assumption into a picture of the future by focusing on the concrete topic of the laboratory: For example, a future of research in which all results are freely available. Or a future of the economy that gets by without international investment.

Another possible approach in this second phase would be for the process facilitator or the participants themselves to work with the assumptions that became visible in the first phase. They could take away important assumptions, add new ones or change the sign. If the participants talked little about technology, a groundbreaking invention may now be inserted. Or the assumption of ongoing globalization may be replaced by the decline of globalization. A third possibility is playful elements, such as "The Thing from the Future" (chapter 14), where strange-looking things are thought up. In any case, the chosen approach should suit the participants: they should be challenged, but not overwhelmed.

In this new, irritating future, the participants deepen their topic. This can happen through a discussion in which further aspects of this future are described, daily life is illuminated, blind spots are filled. They can also describe the path that has led into this future: Which decisions were made by whom, which external influences became important? Or the participants can build a sculpture of their topic in this new future and discuss it. By combining craftsmanship with discussion, one can gain even deeper insights. Or they can depict the future in a role play: Which roles perform which tasks? How are they connected?

This second phase is not easy, but it is theoretically sound and has been tested in practice worldwide. It leads the participants into unfamiliar terrain, to unfamiliar thoughts, and is rather unusual in futures research. Scenario processes also work with different futures. However, these are created by the participants themselves based on the uncertainties they perceive. In the Futures Literacy Labs, the impulse often comes from outside, which allows more irritation and thus more creativity.

New questions emerge

The third phase, the rethink, is then somewhat easier. The participants compare the results of the first two phases and formulate new questions that arise in the present. They are invited to focus on the aspects that caused them particular discomfort, or which are particularly unclear. And on questions that they find difficult to formulate, where they lack concepts or even words. Then the probability is higher that these are truly new questions. If all the others involved understand exactly what is meant by the question, then it may not be that new.

Here too, the collective intelligence of the participants is made visible by first collecting ideas individually and then discussing, refining, and reformulating them in smaller groups. At the end of this phase, the plenary searches for patterns that emerge from the overall collection of questions. And weak signals are pointed out in the questions that perhaps only one person asked. The patterns and the weak signals can then be investigated in depth. Which additional questions might come to the fore? How important good questions are for the competent handling of open futures was described in chapter 2 of this book.

In the fourth phase, next steps or action, concrete projects for the present can be derived from these questions. Who can contribute to answering the questions and how? Who could become active and how? What can politics contribute? In this phase, for example, projects can be developed and put into concrete terms in individual and group work, which are then presented in the plenary.

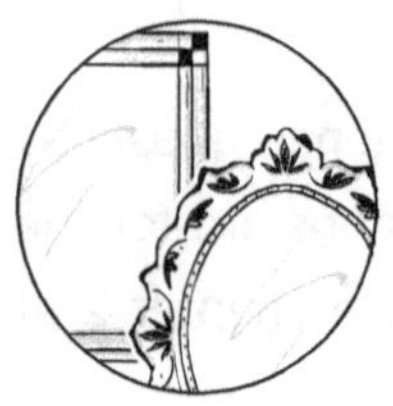

Embracing the openness of the future

My invitation to you is to be aware of the openness of the future and to accept it as a gift.

In your concrete dealings with the future, it can be helpful to imagine alternative, irritating futures of the respective topic. In spring 2020 we all learned what happens if assumptions suddenly do not come true as expected. It was like a big reframe in a huge Futures Literacy Laboratory. A multifaceted approach to the future - a high level of futures literacy - is an important capability for the coming years and decades. You can also set up your own Futures Literacy Labs, just as dozens of organizations around the world have done in recent years.

For reading, I recommend the UNESCO book "Transforming the Future - Anticipation in the 21st Century" mentioned above, and in particular the first and fourth chapters, which deal with the concrete design of the laboratories. For the fifth chapter, I have edited fourteen case studies on topics ranging from sport to youth to innovation. In the seventh chapter, I was able to present our process "Positive Futures – Forum for Frankfurt" as an "Extended Futures Literacy Process". The book is freely accessible online via UNESCO.

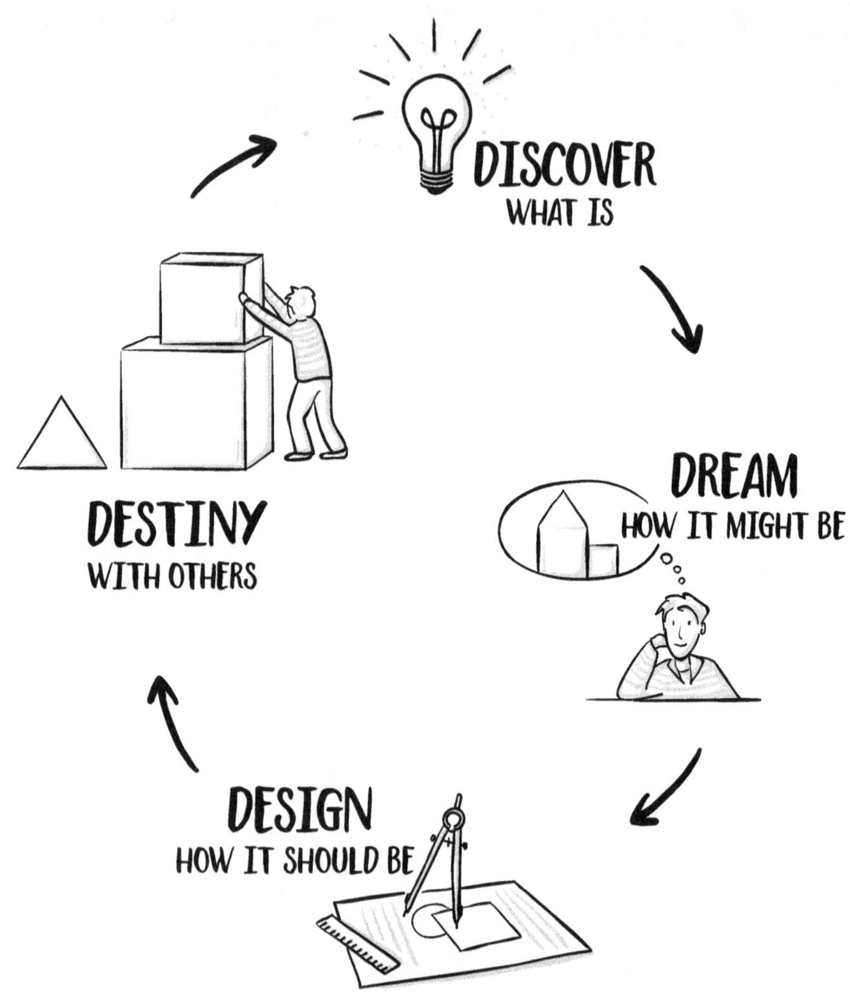

DISCOVER
WHAT IS
DREAM
HOW IT MIGHT BE
DESIGN
HOW IT SHOULD BE
DESTINY
WITH OTHERS

13 Inquire Appreciatively

A visitor from a foundation: "Mr. Bergheim, would you be interested in putting together a group of younger experts and write a report together on the future of the German Social Market Economy?" An exciting, highly relevant topic. But another report by experts? Who would read that? What impact would it have? These were the questions that preoccupied me at the time. The real question behind them: How could a process around a report be designed in such a way that as many perspectives as possible were included, new things could be created, and the results would also have an impact? Which methods could be used when dealing with the future of the social market economy? I outlined my ideas to the person in charge at the foundation, who shortly afterward agreed - for which I am still grateful today - and the process "Future Model of the Social Market Economy" was born.

Involve stakeholders from the beginning

The first change from the originally planned approach was to involve an experienced process designer and facilitator. Process facilitation is much more than moderating events, introducing speakers, and collecting questions from the audience. Rather, its goal is to support a group to develop its full potential and to work successfully as a team. Nina Nisar contributed her knowledge from the global network "Art of Hosting", which is an emerging set of practices for facilitating group conversations of all sizes, supported by principles that maximize collective intelligence. It is an approach to leadership that scales up from the personal to the systemic using personal practice, dialogue, facilitation, and the co-creation of innovation to address complex challenges. It explicitly uses insights from complexity theory and methods such as the Circle, the World Café, Open Space, or Appreciative Inquiry. The latter is presented in this chapter in the context of a concrete process.

The second change arose from the question of who would ultimately do something with the results of our work: Who are the users? Who do we hope would take appropriate action? Can these users be involved in the development of the results? One focus was likely to be on the legal conditions for the economy of the future, so attention quickly turned to members of the German parliament, the Bundestag, and to civil servants in federal ministries.

As originally planned, there was also a core group of experts from various disciplines with two economists, two lawyers, and a cultural scientist. They were joined by a group of professionals with practical experience in the labor market, in a municipality, in business, and in social welfare.

Bringing these different people with their specific experiences and backgrounds together in a process within a year proved to be extremely fruitful. It was not trivial: We could not bring all the people mentioned into one room for two days - as nice as that would have been. Especially for the busy members of the German Bundestag, we needed simpler and shorter engagements. And two days would have been too short anyway to follow up on the ideas and connections that would be created.

Therefore, we decided to approach the different strands of the project side by side and link them together on several occasions. Everything was centrally organized by a small team of two people plus the process facilitator in coordination with the foundation. A researcher was involved in in-depth work, another expert for the preparation and evaluation of the interviews, another process facilitator for the events, and a trend sketcher for the illustration of the reports. A diverse team in which small individual contributions make innovative overall results possible.

What is going well today?

In most cases, projects in Germany and elsewhere start with a problem. Something has not worked properly in the past. The problem must be analyzed and then solved. Often enough it remains open who decided, according to which criteria, that something was not working properly. In any case, problem analysis is usually not much fun anyway, because it is always negative from the outset. Futures orientation is difficult because problems of the past need to be solved.

So why not start with a positive approach: What's going well today? What could be even better tomorrow? Who would have to do what to make more of what is good happen? The method that can do this is the "Appreciative Inquiry", which was developed in the USA in the 1980s. The focus is on looking at existing strengths and potentials. Along the way, it is also made visible who thinks what is "good" and for what reasons. At the same time, there is room to talk about less pleasant topics. These will come up sooner or later anyway, but this aspect does not dominate the general tone of the approach. Cooperrider and Whitney described this method in the book "Appreciative Inquiry - A Positive Revolution in Change" and have used it in many places around the globe. In this way, they identify the positive core of organizations and systems. This core is made visible, appreciated, questioned, and developed further. One starts with what is there and builds ideal worlds that are not detached from current realities.

This method is, as mentioned, a core method of the network "Art of Hosting". I use it in almost every one of my processes and see it as part of the positive wave of the last decades. There are two assumptions behind appreciative inquiry. Firstly, every person, every team, and every organization has great potential, which sometimes already flashes up. Secondly, organizations develop in the direction of what they focus their attention on and what they investigate. In other words, the images they have of the future determine their thinking and actions today. This corresponds to the theory of anticipation.

The method consists of four basic phases, which can be nicely named with four Ds:

1. *Discovery:*

First, successful moments and positive aspects of the respective topic are made visible. The focus is on the question of when something worked particularly well. Ideally, all persons or groups who have a connection to the topic are interviewed. Open interviews are conducted using general guiding questions, i.e. no yes-no answers and no selection from pre-defined lists.

2. *Dream:*

Then the view is directed forward. The interviewees are invited to share their ideas of successful futures. Which futures would they wish for?

3. Design:

In the third step, the preferred futures of the individual interviewees are put together like a mosaic to form a large picture of the diverse future.

4. Destiny:

Then it is time for action to make the vision a reality. It is decided who is involved where and in what way.

Even the labeling of the phases indicates that the transitions are fluid, especially between the more general dream and the more concrete design. Often the first two phases are carried out by many interviewers with even more interview partners. For the third and fourth phases, the interviewers come together and make visible what they have explored.

In the process on the future of the social market economy, for example, the respondents were invited to approach the topic as critics, realists, or visionaries (Walt Disney method). The results of the interviews were then summarized by the interviewers, presented to the core experts to deepen their discussion, presented to the interview partners in Berlin, and published at the end of the process.

The method of Appreciative Inquiry has some connections to other methods of dealing with open futures. Here too, assumptions are made visible, similar to the first phase of a Futures Literacy Laboratory or in dialogue. Here too, it is emphasized that our images of the future have a great influence on our actions today. The step that appreciative inquiry does not take is the examination of an alternative future, the reframing phase in the Futures Literacy Laboratory. This could easily be added as the fifth step before implementation:

"Disrupt" could stimulate the creativity of the participants and let new ideas emerge.

New food for thought

At the beginning of a larger futures process, the most important actors first get to know each other, make their respective experiences and activities visible. The topic is explored, one learns about other actors, explores different sources. This takes time, which fortunately was available here. Two researchers wrote background papers on the historical perspective from the time when the social market economy came into being in Germany in the 1940s and 50s and on the international comparison of social models, which was later helpful in giving rise to new ideas.

At the second meeting of the core group, the first results from the interviews and the background papers were presented. Now, one could feel how the ideas jumped back and forth, how the participants were inspired to formulate new questions and deeper insights. Another place for the emergence of new contexts was the analysis of the interviews together with the authors of the background papers. Here they questioned and connected. Focal points and blind spots became visible. The result of these meetings and further background research was ten thought-provoking impulses for the social market economy. Among other things, the focus was on how societal goals can be formulated more clearly, what effects the dissolution of classic family structures has, how modern communication can be possible in flatter structures, and that specialization cannot be achieved without cooperation.

When is an idea new?

My first major learning from this process about the future of the Social Market Economy is that not many people take time for unfamiliar futures processes with an open outcome. This is completely understandable in terms of systems theory: All potential participants need to ask themselves whether the project helps them to fulfill the tasks in their professional roles. Does the opportunity arise for a scientific research paper? At least for a presentation at a conference? Can I make the interests of my employer visible? If this does not provide sufficient reason for professional participation, private or societal interests could still play a role: Will I enjoy participating? Can I contribute to society? Can I justify this leisure activity against the background of family obligations?

Secondly, the process showed that many people talk about innovation, but it is always difficult to deal with it. If something is really new, then it is impossible for everyone involved to understand what it is about, what the texts mean exactly, and what the connections are. If all this were clear, then the idea cannot be new. It always takes time until societies agree on a commonly shared understanding of a new topic - or until the opposing positions are formulated. Therefore, the design of any futures process should start by addressing the question of how to deal with new questions, issues, concepts, and contexts. Can they serve as food for thought, even if they are not accepted by all sides? Would it be better to use them first internally for further work?

Go out and inquire

Not every futures process can bring together so many different actors in so many different formats. But you can always ask yourself whether there is a way to include a larger variety of perspectives. Probably it is also not possible to switch completely and everywhere from a problem orientation to appreciative inquiry. But you can use individual elements of this approach and gradually increase their importance.

> **How can as many perspectives as possible be connected? Which formats are particularly suitable?**

You can design your events as processes of collective intelligence knowledge creation. At events organized by others, you could point out possibly missing perspectives and alternative methodological possibilities.

> **Why not use appreciative inquiry in your own private or professional context?**

If you want to go one step further, you can also take part in an Art of Hosting training to learn more about Appreciative Inquiry, process design, and other methods. The book "Appreciative Inquiry. A positive revolution in change" was written by David Cooperrider and Diana Whitney.

 14 Discover the Future in a Playful Way

A loft in an old building in Berlin-Kreuzberg on a hot summer evening in 2018. In one corner of the room, people are pondering strategic issues. In another corner, people are laughing out loud. In between, one group is concerned with the role of compassion, and another with the importance of stamina in societal transformation. I had the pleasure to bring these different groups together in one room for the book presentation of Riel Miller's "Transforming the Future". Martin Ciesielski had the laughs on his side that evening. He used to work in the banking industry, like me, and now, as a business jester, he encourages people to think more deeply with humor and improvisational theater. For him, as the founder of the "School of

Nothing", one starting point is the exploration of nothingness. In this way, he enables people with hands, hearts, and minds to work together. At the "Futures Literacy Design Forum" at the UNESCO headquarters in Paris in late 2019, Martin invited participants to depict various forms of behavior in social sculptures and as mini theater plays. According to the improvisational motto "let the others shine", the participants worked appreciatively with what they had consciously and unconsciously brought with them.

Model the future yourself

Martin's approach fits in wonderfully with the many different paths that are taken in futures work around the world to go beyond the analytical approach. For example, participants in larger Futures Literacy Laboratories are regularly invited to present their various futures as sculptures. From a collection of different materials, they can choose what they want to model individual elements of their future. In small groups, they talk to each other about what these elements represent and why, and how this might fit in with the other parts of the jointly created sculpture. The result is rarely comprehensible to outsiders. That is not necessary. What is crucial is that the participants gain further access to the topic of the event by working with their hands, that they inspire each other and discover something new.

Another way to discover the future is to play cards. This can be very enjoyable and lead to unexpected results, as the participants of a small Futures Literacy Laboratory on the future of journalism were able to experience. In the reframe phase of the laboratory, I gave them the card game "The Thing from the Future", which Stuart

Candy had developed with colleagues. With three times 34 cards, it allows for unusual combinations of sentences like "In a bright future of journalism, there is a building related to war. What is it?" or "In a wise future of journalism, there is a tool related to water. What is it?". In three places these two sentences and nearly 40,000 other combinations of the game differ. The small difference unleashes a great deal of creativity in group work and is a lot of fun. Above all, it allows for new perspectives on the possible futures of the topic. Since mid-2020, thanks to Greek programmers, the game can be played in Minecraft in a slightly modified version.

Meanwhile, there are more card games. The AKAW Futures Card Game created by Christian Rauch uses trends, technologies, perspectives, and ideation to foster creative discussions. The Future Game 2050 offers different roles - like the bee counter or the AI warden - from whose perspectives the future can then be viewed.

There are also board games of the future. In the game "Stranger Futures" by the Polish futurists around Norbert Kolos, the starting point is a list of assumptions about the respective topic, which were created, for example, in an earlier phase of a futures process. These assumptions are then challenged, changed, or reinforced by the players. For convincing ideas, players receive chips, which are counted at the end. A winner can be determined. Existing assumptions are challenged, and new assumptions are made during the game. These can then be used in the next steps of a longer process.

The Polak game, named after the Dutch sociologist Frederik Lodewijk Polak, is relatively simple and can be used at the beginning of events. Here, the participants first position themselves in the room along a line according to whether they are optimistic or pessimistic about the future of the topic under investigation. From there, the second dimension is opened up: The participants show whether they see the future as largely predetermined or whether they see considerable human creative freedom. In this way, a lot of assumptions quickly become visible, and it is possible to get to know the people in the room better.

Describe power through a game

The Indian mystic P.R. Sarkar developed a game that works with four types of power: The power of workers, warriors, intellectuals, and capitalists. The workers want income and security. If they are dissatisfied, they can bring chaos and confusion. The warriors strive for order and loyalty. With the power of their weapons, they can dominate their environment. The intellectuals want truth and clarity. With the power of their ideas, they can create alternative futures. Finally, the capitalists want to achieve material growth and have the power of money.

Participants are divided into these four groups and given descriptions of their roles and corresponding symbols such as shovels, weapons, books, or money. First, the workers investigate the topic at hand and create a future according to their tastes. Then, step by step, the other groups join in and challenge the future created so far by bringing in their value systems. One can imagine that it quickly becomes confusing. Just like in societal practice. The crucial thing is that after the game participants discuss what happened in it.

There are hardly any limits to imagining futures. On the one hand regarding the variety of futures, but also regarding the ways to explore them playfully. It seems important to me that the playful elements are cleverly integrated into a larger process. They can help with warming up and getting to know each other. Through fun and laughter, they can contribute to an atmosphere that allows for more creativity. And they can provide even more depth, new connections, new insights, which dialogue or discussion with words alone may not be able to create.

Play with the future

This chapter has shown you some of the ways to approach futures topics playfully.

> **Try some of them or completely different ones. Perhaps first for a warm-up at a larger event. Or with a smaller group as part of a longer process. Take advantage of the experience of people who have been intensively involved in games for a long time.**

If you want to read more about "The Thing from the Future", I recommend chapter 6 in the book "Transforming the Future - Anticipation in the 21st Century". An introduction to the Sarkar Game is provided in Sohail Inayatullah's article "Using Gaming to Understand the Patterns of the Future - The Sarkar Game in Action" from 2013. The websites of the other persons and organizations mentioned in this chapter contain further suggestions.

15 Digital Tools for Futures

A posh conference center in the Taunus mountains outside Frankfurt in spring 2013. I am invited to enrich a meeting of organizational developers with my perspectives. Our host asks me about topics related to progress, change, and leadership. The listeners are attentive and prepare their questions. So far so conventional. But they type their questions into their smartphones. And they rate the questions of the other participants. We discussants then choose which of the questions we want to answer or where we want to ask back. Back then, I first encountered what is now a common way of interacting with participants, students, and staff. Since then, I have been looking for digital tools that can improve work on open futures. And I try to use them in my processes wherever it makes sense. The Corona times have accelerated this development considerably.

Digital tools are always useful when they make something possible that cannot be achieved in direct, personal encounters. Or when this direct encounter is not accessible due to geographical distances or other restrictions. Above all, these tools can and should make visible the collective intelligence of the participants in a room and outside. At the event in the Taunus mountains, all participants had the chance to enter a question. Without digital support, a few, usually more extroverted people often dominate such question rounds. But to develop new ideas for the big issues of the present, we also need the insights and questions of the doubters, the silent ones, the introverts. We allow diversity, open the discussion and invite the seldom-heard voices.

It worked well back then. Everyone was in the same room. Almost everyone had the necessary technical equipment. There was direct feedback to their input into the computer. But only the people in the room were reached. It is nice when many people can get involved in a dialogue process in this way. Especially people who do not have the time or money to go to an evening event in the local town hall, for example.

Digital tools can also be used to exclude people. Some don't have the technical infrastructure, others don't have the competency to handle the technology. Still others do not want to use such a medium to discuss important societal issues. And some view certain applications critically or reject them on data protection grounds. So, you should think carefully about which target group you want to reach and by what means. And one should consider what compromises must be made in the quality of the dialogue. Direct exchange is now also possible for large groups with several sub-groups via video conferences. But then everyone must be in the online room at the same time. If you want to reach even more people at a time that suits them individually, feedback will be difficult or should be well organized over a longer period. It is important to combine digital and analog tools smartly.

Ask questions

Futures work usually begins with a topic and a question: What does a city worth living in look like? Which health care systems are possible? Or: How could social cohesion continue? Then these general questions are often broken down into smaller, feasible elements and used as an introduction to the discussions. That is why it is important in the digital space not only to collect the questions of the participants - as happened back then in the Taunus. Rather, it is also important to ask questions yourself and to bring the answers together in the process. Some apps may have to be handled in a somewhat flexible way to allow free text answers to specific questions. And the analysis can be much more difficult. Therefore, additional facilitation and research resources are needed to look at the answers and, if necessary, link them to the offline discussion. It is also possible to take the results into the next steps of a longer process. At a large event in Berlin as part of our dialogue process #gutlebendigital, we were able to combine both.

Online forms are an easy way to gather the perspectives of many people. The more people participate and the more open the questions are, the more time and effort it will take to ask back or give feedback on the answers. But that applies offline as well. In the German Chancellor's Futures Dialogue in 2011/12, so many people participated via the process's website that additional staff had to be brought in.

A good measure of transparency

There are some challenges to the content and technical design of the questionnaires. If the questions are very personal and the answers are publicly available, then only a small group of people will participate: People with a clear world view and a high urge to articulate it. In the process on the future of Frankfurt, we received only a few answers online to the question of what is important to people in life. All those answers were made visible on the website with the name of the respondent. In retrospect, this was not a good decision. Offline, this question had brought a lot of valuable insights.

In #gutlebendigital, we made the answers of the participants in our digital survey only available to the project team. Nobody else saw that, for example, one participant made a profound statement in a long text about where digitalization is already making a positive contribution to quality of life. Thus, no online exchange with other participants could take place. The project team, however, went into the exchange. And we invited the participants with the most valuable insights to a face-to-face event in Frankfurt - where again not everyone could come.

Since 2020 I have been able to facilitate several online Futures Literacy Laboratories. For this purpose, we use a video platform and, for the harvesting of the results, an application that is simultaneously accessible and editable by all participants. It is a joy to see how the collective intelligence of the group becomes visible quite quickly when everyone enters their elements of desirable futures at the same time. Valuable results can be achieved without the need for travel.

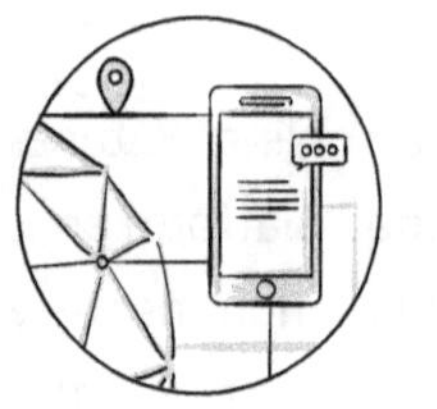

Organize community

In larger, longer-term futures processes, it is also a matter of organizing the community.

Who became involved in the process, when, through what channels, and how? Who should be involved in the future? Who knows whom? Who are the contact persons for special topics? How do you keep them all up to date?

Client Relationship Management (CRM) systems are available to help answer these questions. In the Frankfurt dialogue process, Nationbuilder enabled us to reach significantly more people than we would have been able to without it. With appropriate permission, we created entries in the database for all contact persons. The registration for larger events was handled through this, as were the online surveys. Newsletters were then sent out from the database. At that time, we even used the interfaces to Facebook and Twitter: every reaction to one of our posts there was recorded in the Nationbuilder database. However, this was of little value to the process at the time and from today's perspective it is highly questionable from a data-ethical point of view.

Meanwhile, there is an almost unmanageable number of platforms and tools for collaboration in the digital space. Trade fairs and large events such as the 2020 "High-Level Futures Literacy Summit" are organized online under the influence of Covid-19 as are small team meetings. A comprehensive presentation of this variety is not the aim of this chapter. Rather, it is intended to offer suggestions for cleverly combining online and onsite encounters in futures processes. Make good use of the options and also consider the limits of the online world.

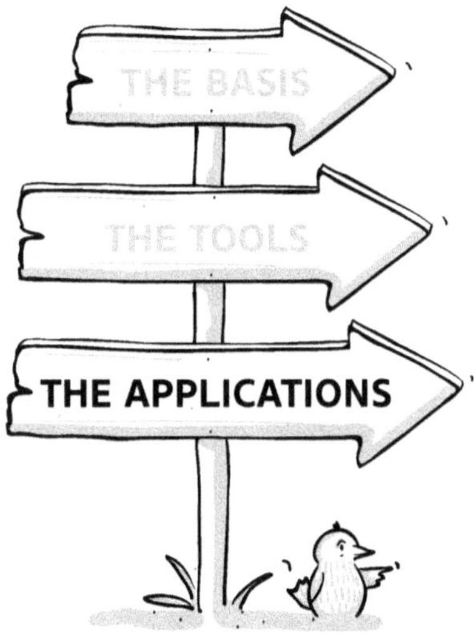

THE BASIS
THE TOOLS
THE APPLICATIONS

16 Futures Dialogue of the German Chancellor

A cold January day in Berlin in 2012. Today I am meeting the host of one of the best dialogue processes I have ever been involved in: German Chancellor Angela Merkel. I will present to her the initial proposals of my working group on "Prosperity, Quality of Life and Progress" in her "Dialogue on Germany's Future". She had asked us to draw up proposals on how to develop a meaningful and shared image of a desirable future for Germany and how to find better measures for quality of life. The Chancellor is an excellent listener, asks questions, draws connections. She didn't tell us what was not possible - even though various restrictions on her freedom of action also became visible - but encouraged us to make the proposals more precise and then include them in the final report.

Great variety of voices

One reason for my continued enthusiasm for this dialogue on the future is the extraordinarily colorful mix of topics and people brought together here by the Chancellery. Identifying and inviting participants is one of the major and non-trivial tasks for all organizers of futures processes. In the group which I was allowed to lead as the core expert, there were participants with a focus on social, economic, labor, and environmental issues. They came from universities, an international organization, a social association, and civil society. However: only men. In the other 17 groups of the expert dialogue, each with eight to ten participants, there were more women, and the variety of backgrounds was even greater: among others, the director of the Federal Centre for Health Education, a school director, a tax lawyer, a chief commissioner, the managing director of a job center and a community organizer were involved.

But there was even more variety. In parallel to the expert dialogue, citizens were invited to take part in an online dialogue to express their opinions on the same questions that we experts were addressing. This invitation was accepted by far more people than originally expected in the Chancellery. Almost 12,000 suggestions for future government action were made and 74,000 comments were added. Many of the proposals showed a high level of commitment from citizens and a great deal of knowledge about societal issues. At the same time, it became apparent that some groups are extremely well organized online and can activate a lot of support. The proposals to legalize cannabis were voted on high in the polls, making an issue visible that would later become politically relevant in many countries. In addition to the online dialogue, there were three citizens' talks between the Chancellor and 100 participants as well as several small events.

Clear structure, powerful questions

The second reason for my continued enthusiasm about this futures dialogue is the clear structure and powerful questions that were asked at the beginning. First, the three guiding questions of the three strands of topics: How do we want to live together? How do we want to make a living? How do we want to learn? These questions selected by the host are of great relevance and not all answers are known yet. Also, the 18 working groups received further questions and were asked to describe where Germany stands on their topic today, what trends they expect to see in five to ten years and what the Federal Government can do during this period. Specific questions for each working group were derived from this. In my group, these were: What is prosperity, and what is societal progress? How do we achieve a society-wide understanding of prosperity and quality of life? What measures of success and prosperity do we need to measure quality of life? And: What do institutions in politics and science look like with which complex cross-sectional and long-term issues can be constructively addressed together? By discussing the various questions, a common understanding of the task was reached, and experts got to know each other.

When such powerful questions are asked, the path to good ideas and proposals for action is well prepared. In addition, there was neutral process facilitation from outside the Chancellery, which was helpful for the quality and focus of the discussions. And there were no prohibitions to think, no desired answers from the host's point of view. The task was "merely" to develop proposals for action for federal policy, for which great societal need was seen and which should be realizable within a time horizon of five to ten years. We were explicitly invited to think laterally, to think differently, to think anew. And we were to make visible expected areas of tension and conflicts. We were also asked to include the citizens' proposals in our considerations.

Relevance for action

At the same time, it was also clear that the proposals would not be cast into law one-to-one, but that the Chancellor would choose what to pursue. In August 2012 I was back in the Federal Chancellery for the presentation of the proposals of all working groups and to present the final report. To my great pleasure, the Chancellery had drawn up a list of 24 proposals that were to be pursued with the aim of implementation. This was a clear sign of the appreciation and relevance of our work. My joy was even greater when I found two proposals from my working group on the list: The Citizens' Dialogue on Quality of Life "Vision 2040 - for my Children" and the "Progress Report on Quality of Life" as a regular and interdepartmental statement by the Federal Government on the most important policy areas relating to quality of life. I was also pleased with the high quality of many of the proposals from the other working groups. They ranged from an individual competency passport to a Germany-wide health monitor and the simplification of citizen participation to the idea of an International German Forum. Ten citizens' proposals were also selected and followed up by the Chancellery. These included, for example, a national cleanup day, a joint online portal for German science & education, and the amendment of the law on care for the elderly.

All in all, the variety of participants, the powerful questions, the clear structure, and the prominent, influential host made a strong process possible with innovative recommendations for action. There was a clear division of tasks between the hosts, who provided the rooms and the organization, the process facilitators, who structured and facilitated individual events, and us participants, who contributed their content. This separation of tasks was helpful but differs from many other processes, where the hosts often also facilitate and determine content at the same time. And this was not an abstract discussion outside the system, but with parts of the political system and with the hope of concrete application of the results.

A small group

The process was initiated and supported by a small group in the Federal Chancellery with a key person who was the source of the idea, who was able to gain support from the very top, and who was strongly committed to the core of the process: Andrea Schneider, then Deputy Head of the Policy Planning Staff. Her example shows what is possible when you try something new and gather supporters for it.

I like to think that I too have made a small contribution to the development of this groundbreaking process. After all, I had previously presented my report on futures studies for states at the Chancellery, in which I had promoted "broad-based, open, inter-disciplinary and interdepartmental communication processes". And I had brought Riel Miller, the current Head of Futures Literacy at

UNESCO, and the Finnish complexity expert Mika Aaltonen to the Chancellery for meetings. Both had pleaded for a broad and open discussion of futures.

Limits of the process

Despite all the respect for what has been achieved in the Future Dialogue, the limits of the process must not be concealed. For example, the quality of the dialogue did not always meet the high standards of dialogue that specialists such as David Bohm or William Isaacs formulated (chapter 1). But talking to each other in a circle without a leader, without an agenda, without a goal, was not the appropriate format here. But then: A few years later, some of the workshops of the 2nd International German Forum did not take place around the heavy tables in the conference rooms, but in circles of chairs in the broad corridors of the Chancellery.

A greater challenge for the subsequent implementation of the results was the fact that the federal ministries were not involved in the dialogue. In theory, a dialogue process should involve all those who are later implementing the proposals. At first glance, such a dialogue procedure is not compatible with the interministerial principle of Article 65 of the German Basic Law and the ministries' claims to autonomy. This is where I saw a major task for the future: to make a generative dialogue possible at this level as well.

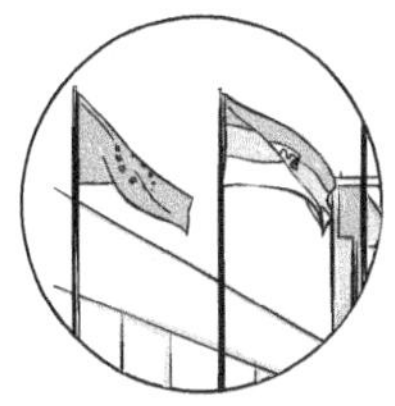

Initiate futures dialogues yourself

For any futures dialogue, support from the very top is helpful. This does not have to and cannot always be the Federal Chancellor, Prime Minister, or President. In every company or every association, some topics can be approached with a structure similar to the one presented here. In this way similarly rich results are possible. This will not happen without effort. It takes time outside of the day-to-day business. And it needs a small group of people to structure and drive the process.

This chapter should encourage you to initiate a small dialogue process about the future in your context. In the other chapters of the book, there are further suggestions. If you would like to learn more about the Chancellor's Dialogue on Germany's Future, you can read the freely accessible report on the results of the Expert Dialogue.

 17 Futures of Cities

The importance of combining thinking and doing became clear to me once again in June 2013 on the podium in the Federal Chancellery. At Chancellor Merkel's 1st International German Forum on "What matters to people – wellbeing and progress", I had just spoken about how important spaces for dialogue are where different people and groups can have a say, express their ideas about quality of life and work together to improve it. I called upon my audience to be hosts for such spaces, to be open to the content that might emerge, and to commit themselves to the implementation of selected results. What I could not know at the time, not even dare to dream: At the end of 2013, the federal government's coalition agreement would state exactly that: "We want to orient our government actions more closely to the values and objectives of our citizens and are therefore conducting a dialogue with them about their understanding of quality of life. "

Do it yourself

What I knew at that time: I would not be able to place my ideas in any higher place in Germany. An important part of the work at the Center for Societal Progress was done. What next? Do it myself! Not only give other people or organizations smart advice but do it myself. Why not in Frankfurt? The first preliminary work had already been done since the Council of Ideas of the Progress Centre had expressed an "All politics is local" and a small group on the future of the city had formed in Frankfurt. And in our publication series "Positive Futures" we had examined in detail several dialogue projects aimed at improving the quality of life at the local and regional level: Jacksonville in Florida, Santa Cruz in California, and Tasmania in Australia.

So in late 2013, I was sitting in the rooms of an Islamic cultural association in the small center of Frankfurt's Nordweststadt. A district with great challenges. Diagonally opposite, the staff of the Ark takes care of disadvantaged children during the day. Ben Warner from Jacksonville had told me that a project about the future of a city should be active precisely in such districts. So, I told some people about our project. A Muslim co-advisor in our kindergarten then gave me the telephone number of the chairman of this cultural association: "Call him! He is nice." True. We explained to him and his colleagues in the cultural association who we were and what we were doing. And step by step we got into a conversation about quality of life in Nordweststadt. It became particularly apparent how much importance they attached to peaceful coexistence and to education. They were already active on peacefully living together. On the other hand, we heard about helplessness and powerlessness in the field of education, which was to become an important impulse in the process "Positive Futures - Forum for Frankfurt" (Schöne Aussichten – Forum für Frankfurt).

Variety through many small events

After this successful start, the team from Positive Futures managed to set up further small events in the station mission, with long-term unemployed, with young parents, with children and young people, with senior citizens, or with immigrants. Everywhere we had the impression that people were happy that someone was interested in them and their lives, was listening to them. There were also several large events in town halls. In addition, there was the possibility to participate online.

And we held bilateral talks with influential people in the city center. All in all, we managed to achieve a good mix in this volunteering project, which largely met the high standards of Ben Warner from Jacksonville: Everyone in Frankfurt should be able to get the impression that "someone like him/her" was involved in the project. This is a standard that I have since then also set for other projects that are better equipped financially and in terms of personnel.

This dialogue phase was the first step in the quality-of-life process "Positive Futures - Forum for Frankfurt". In the second step, the results were summarized into visions: Which images of desirable futures became visible? In the third step, suitable indicators were sought with which to check where the gap between vision and reality is still particularly large. In the end, projects and actions were identified and launched to reduce this gap. All this was done for the ten topics of work & business, leisure, art & culture, education, health & wellbeing, environment, transport & mobility, housing, living together & belonging, security, and politics & administration.

Dialogue, Visions, Indicators, Action

In the dialogue phase, we relied heavily on the method of Appreciative Inquiry (chapter 13) and on questions from the processes in Jacksonville, Santa Cruz, and Tasmania. The four initial questions were: 1. What is important to you personally in your life? Thus, the personal level of the interviewees was addressed. 2. What constitutes a high quality of life in Frankfurt for you? This was intended to help us make the move from the individual to the city level. 3. What hurts your heart when you think of Frankfurt? With this question, the negative aspects should also be made visible, even if this contradicts the basic idea of an appreciative inquiry. And: 4. Frankfurt in 15 years: What changes do you wish for? Even if this was formally the only question with a futures perspective, in retrospect it was the weakest question that brought few new insights.

We heard a lot about the topic of living together. The vision text does not sound surprising. However, it makes aspects visible that are not yet in place from the point of view of the people in Frankfurt:

"In the year 2030, Frankfurt am Main is a city in which respectful coexistence of all people is part of everyday life. Recognition, appreciation, and consideration are made possible and promoted through meetings, dialogue, and exchange in public life, at home, and in the neighborhood. Encounters, civic engagement, and helpfulness are natural parts of life. Newcomers feel welcome and appreciated. People respect and help each other, and members of different generations live together. Everyone can take part in social life regardless of their individual background".

The indicators for this topic pointed to considerable potential for improvement: Trust in fellow human beings was lower than in other major German cities. Neighbors did not help each other as much as desired. Foreigners and senior citizens were not well integrated into urban society. There was not even any data on the integration of people with disabilities. Correspondingly, the projects that were to improve the situation in the fourth step all had a connection to living together: The neighborhood parties, the living room travels, and the repair cafés.

The value of quality-of-life processes

The added value of such a quality-of-life process lies in at least two places: Firstly, it enables encounters between different people, thematic fields, and projects that would otherwise not come together. At our large events, we were able to bring people from different districts, age groups, and educational biographies into a conversation. Regularly participants were surprised that other people were interested in similar topics as they. That connects. Linkages across topics also became visible. The topic of mobility, for example, is often only discussed among mobility experts, without considering closely related topics such as work and housing. In Positive Futures, this work on cross-cutting issues took place primarily through the close collaboration between the ten topic hosts within the team. All the hosts discussed all dialogue results, all visions, all indicators. Fortunately, we had not followed an impulse during the initial phase. At that time, it was considered whether we should limit ourselves to one topic area or one district of the city. We decided to cover all topics and the city overall. However, we drew the system border at the city limits, which with hindsight was a severe restriction given the many connections with the surrounding area. Such compromises in the design are part of every futures process.

Secondly, the indicators have improved the information base for various actors. It would have been nice if the city government had taken a position on the indicators and formally aligned its own actions to them. However, this is not realistic, as it is too restrictive for politicians. Change does not work that mechanically. Nevertheless, we had the impression that half a year after the indicators were published, several projects were launched that addressed the focus indicators from "Positive Futures" such as cleanliness, noise, or cohesion. All these issues are still highly relevant today.

Challenges on the way

During the overall process, several challenges became apparent which could probably also occur in other futures processes and which should not be swept under the carpet here. Some powerful people saw no need for such a process, as they had the legal legitimacy or the necessary knowledge to make Frankfurt a more livable city. We informed these people about the course of the process but did not expect any support from them. Also, some existing projects hoped that "Positive Futures" would be a marketing platform for them and their ideas about the future. When they realized that it would instead be about working together, appreciating different perspectives, and making connections, some of these projects withdrew from the process.

Due to the limited resources of time and money, we were not able to involve as many people and launch as many projects as we would have liked. Every process has limits. And every process is always just one of many building blocks in actively shaping the future.

Talk to others about the futures of your city

Wherever possible, involve people outside the usual circles in discussions on important issues or insist that this be done by politicians and administrators.

You could also check the indicators of quality of life in your city for their relevance and completeness - perhaps in a small salon with other people. Just because certain data are published, they are not necessarily relevant for your future. And maybe there are blind spots in the published indicators. Go on a search.

And why not tackle these four steps in your city with other people: Dialogue, vision, indicators, action. For further reading, I recommend the freely accessible results from "Positive Futures - Forum for Frankfurt" and the general overview of the process in "Quality-of-life processes – A Manual". Also, there is my chapter 7 in "Transforming the Future" on "An extended Futures Literacy Process - Design lessons from measuring wellbeing".

18 Government Strategy Wellbeing in Germany

A warm September evening in the lower section of Berlin's central railway station. I am waiting for the train that will take me home to Frankfurt am Main after a long session in the Federal Chancellery. The homeless´ newspaper "Road Sweeper" (Straßenfeger) is offered. I pay and to my great delight, I discover on the front page three people who focus on the topic of social cohesion. Inside the paper, I find more pictures of people who address questions about quality of life. Those pictures were taken at an event of the "Permanent Representation of Street Children" at the Academy for Co-Determination in Jamlitz, Brandenburg. As part of the dialogue process of the government strategy "Wellbeing in Germany", civil servants from the German government and trained facilitators went there to talk with the young people about what is important to them personally in life and what, in their opinion, constitutes quality of life in Germany.

Variety across Germany

How splendid! In the Chancellor's Futures Dialogue we had proposed a wellbeing dialogue and in our process "Positive Futures - Forum for Frankfurt" we had had good experiences in dialogue with seldom-heard voices. As a member of the scientific advisory board of the government strategy "Wellbeing in Germany", I had reported on these experiences and repeatedly emphasized the value of open dialogue with as many different people as possible. The process team in the Federal Chancellery took up these impulses with impressive consistency. They also organized dialogues with the Joblinge Leipzig, in two nursing homes in Wünsdorf and Stralsund, in a school for the hearing impaired and deaf in Bad Camberg and at SC Rollstuhlsport München. This involved a lot of work for the Chancellery. Therefore, the term "difficult-to-reach groups" was used there. Later I did not hear from anyone who did not consider the effort and the encounters to be important and valuable.

There were some doubts in advance. For some employees of the federal ministries involved in the process, this was an unfamiliar procedure. They saw the politicians in the cities and districts as being responsible for picking up the signals from the population. At the same time, they also saw that this was working less and less well. Some scientists saw no real need for this dialogue and pointed to the large number of scientific reports and surveys about quality of life. My enthusiasm for dialogues and outreach work has continued to grow during "Wellbeing in Germany". People want to be seen and heard. They have something to say. And it is possible to summarize the variety of the results in an overall picture.

There was a total of more than 200 dialogue events, three of them with the Federal Chancellor in Rostock, Duisburg-Marxloh, and Nuremberg, and about 50 with federal ministers. The population was also able to answer the two questions online and via postcards: What do you think is important in life? What, in your opinion, is characteristic of the quality of life in Germany? In addition to these two questions, which we had also asked in "Positive Futures - Forum for Frankfurt", they did not ask: What hurts your heart when you think about Germany? This would presumably have provided further valuable insights, but at the same time, it would also have risked turning the mood into a negative one. A total of almost 16,000 people took part in this dialogue. That is only a small percentage of Germany's more than 80 million inhabitants. But it was more than in most other governmental processes. The invitation to participate was extended through a wide range of channels. The requirement of Ben Warner from Jacksonville was largely fulfilled: The great diversity of the population was included as much as possible.

High quality dialogue

Also, the quality of the dialogue at most of the events was high thanks to the clever design and professional process facilitation, which I was able to experience as an observer on four occasions. As a rule, the participants sat together in small groups in which everyone had their say. Moderator cards were used where everyone could write their answers, and which were then made visible in the plenary. The most important topics were deepened in the second part of the events. In the official documentation of the government strategy, there are photo protocols, lists of events, photos of the postcards, and other items.

The many thousands of responses were then compiled by external experts using a mixture of qualitative and quantitative content analysis. With the help of computers, they developed a category system with 17 categories such as work, culture, family, and tolerance and 160 subcategories. They documented this wealth in a publicly accessible report, which we discussed several times on the scientific advisory board.

Relevant indicators

In the next step, 48 indicators were found in collaboration among all federal ministries, matching the results from the public dialogue. These indicators should "draw attention to critical developments at an early stage and thus identify potential fields of action for policymakers", as the final report states. The result is one of the best indicator systems at the national level that I know of - even if for me some indicators raise questions (what does the old-age dependency ratio say?) and others seem to be missing (perhaps the illiteracy rate or the number of suicides). Fortunately, however, many important indicators have been made visible. For example, the proportion of people who say they can get help from others if necessary. Or the perceived ability of citizens to influence politics, the commuting time, and the prevalence of obesity. The presentation in the interactive report on the government's website, where some indicators can also be viewed by region and in international comparison, is particularly impressive.

The Federal Government had thus achieved much of what was agreed in the coalition agreement of 2013 on the subject of quality of life: "We want to orient our government actions more closely to the values and objectives of our citizens and are therefore conducting a dialogue with them about their understanding of quality of life. [...] On this basis, we will develop an indicator and reporting system on quality of life in Germany." However, the next step for action was not taken as consistently as envisaged in the coalition agreement: "We want to incorporate the findings into an interdepartmental action plan "live well" to improve the quality of life in Germany."

Hurdles on the way

Such an action plan was never published. Nor were the 48 indicators ranked by priorities for future action: Which issues require special attention, need additional time, and financial resources? Perhaps some ministers and their staff felt that the strict structure of "Dialogue - Indicators - Action" limited their freedom of decision too much. Perhaps they also feared long-term negative effects if they failed in improving the indicators. Or they recognized that in many cases, laborious cooperation with other ministries would have been necessary to generate lasting improvements.

After the end of my work on the government strategy's scientific advisory board, I compiled ten important indicators that should receive more societal attention because Germany is not in a good position compared to its aspirations - as had become visible in the dialogue - or compared to other countries: It would be important to increase voter turnout, make housing cheaper, strengthen the feeling of security, promote trust in fellow human beings, reduce the number of suicides, reduce obesity and lower the ecological footprint. In all these areas, close cooperation between the government, business, and civil society, between the federal, state, and local governments, and between different ministries and research fields is probably necessary. The potential for dialogue is huge.

Optimistically, I assume that the experiences and results from the dialogue phase and the development of indicators of the government strategy have had an impact at various points and will continue to do so. All employees of the federal ministries who traveled to the public dialogues took home impressions. All participants in the dialogues could apply this practice in their context. Perhaps the indicators will also be used in some ministries as a starting point for setting their priorities without discussing them externally. Rarely can changes in complex social systems be causally attributed to individual events or processes. Different influences often come together. For example, I was pleased that a major political party moved into the 2017 federal election campaign with the slogan "For a country where we live well and happily" and thus carried the issue of quality of life further.

In my view, three factors were decisive for the success of the government strategy and, in principle, of all dialogue processes: firstly, a neutral host with high visibility, own resources, and, at the same time, complete openness concerning content. Secondly, a great diversity of participants. And thirdly, professional external process facilitators.

Dialogue processes in your context

Not every dialogue process can be as large and visible as a government strategy. But in small processes dialogue can be practiced, connections can be made, and new insights can become visible. In this way, the collective intelligence in organizations, cities, or the country is strengthened. This is how trust is built, communication takes place, meaning is developed. Feel encouraged and invited to promote this in your context.

Those who would like to take a closer look at the process and results of the government strategy will find a wealth of information at gut-leben-in-deutschland.de/en/.

19 Shaping Digitalization

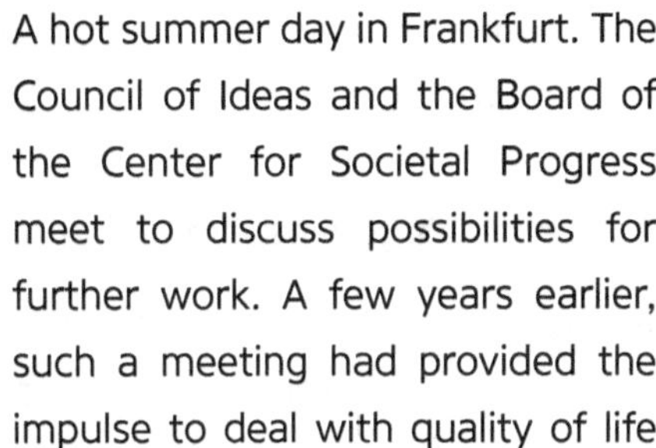

A hot summer day in Frankfurt. The Council of Ideas and the Board of the Center for Societal Progress meet to discuss possibilities for further work. A few years earlier, such a meeting had provided the impulse to deal with quality of life at the municipal level, which later led to the process "Positive Futures - Forum for Frankfurt". This time the impulse went in a different direction. "Wouldn't it be time to look at the rapid development of digitalization from the point of view of quality-of-life research?" asked Jan Hofmann, physicist, futurist, and, as an employee of a large telecommunications company, deeply involved in digitalization. Digitalization is defined here as the increasing generation and use of data for communication with and between machines.

Connect discourses

Indeed, when we asked people about their needs and visions of the future in "Positive Futures", digitalization issues were hardly ever mentioned. Even in the government strategy "Wellbeing in Germany", there was hardly any talk of digitalization beyond the expansion of broadband. The topic also had little visibility in scientific quality-of-life research. At the same time, the number of users of digital platforms rose rapidly. Their providers promised that our lives would become better by using their products. How exactly this was supposed to happen, I found few clear statements and few reliable facts. So, it was time to bring the discourses together, to offer a bridge. We wanted to look at quality of life through the digitalization lens and at the same time, we wanted to look at digitalization through the quality-of-life lens. All this with the methodology of the Center for Societal Progress: Dialogue - Vision - Indicators - Action. The process #gutlebendigital (roughly: living well digitally) was born.

It was an ambitious plan, for which we needed partners, supporters, and comrades-in-arms. Ideally, partners would incorporate the results into their actions. We knocked on the doors of big technology companies from Germany and abroad. We contacted associations, foundations, and federal ministries. From the discussions with individual employees, a great deal of interest became apparent: Yes, such a dialogue process would be enormously important and there is currently no place where this connection is being made. However, at no point was it possible to obtain a greater contribution to the process from the respective organizations. This was probably not due to the individuals involved.

Challenge of openness

My guess is that the openness of the process in terms of content was not acceptable for those organizations. I could not and did not want to guarantee that the results would fit the thematic and economic priorities of each organization. I could not convince them that it might be important for them too to hear what the priorities of the population are in this topic - beyond the usual questionnaires and market research. Just as the Federal Chancellor had listened to the population in her futures processes with an open mind. All attempts were in vain. That did not stop us from carrying out the process nevertheless, with our limited resources.

In two dialogue phases in 2017/18, we invited people to discuss in 20 events, 20 one-on-one interviews, and an online questionnaire how digitalization can be designed in such a way that it has the greatest possible positive impact on people's quality of life. Based on the results, the #gutlebendigital team developed visions for eleven topic areas, identified 28 suitable indicators and more than 50 projects that make the desirable future more likely. Everything was accompanied by a blog, a website, a newsletter, and social media activities. The results were published in freely accessible form on gutlebendigital.de also in English.

The method used during the dialogue phase was based on Appreciative Inquiry, with four questions: Where do you currently see the positive effects of digitalization on people's quality of life? In which areas does digitalization not yet have the hoped-for impact on quality of life or even negative consequences? Please describe an ideal future from your point of view: Where and how does digitalization have a positive effect on quality of life? And: Who would have to do what to move us towards this ideal future?

Involve many disciplines

In this process, too, it was important to ensure the greatest possible diversity of participants. We were able to hold events with software developers, entrepreneurs, organizational developers, human resources managers, students, communication experts, real estate experts, ministry employees, pensioners, social workers, and others. In the individual interviews, we were able to talk to people from the scientific disciplines of philosophy, theology, ethics, linguistics, psychology, sociology, political science, computer science, and also with founders and activists.

All of them had a great interest and some experience at the interface of digitalization and quality of life. We would have liked to increase the diversity even more with events in rural areas and by talking to people who are less educated or less involved in digitalization. We would also have liked to bring the different actors more into contact with each other instead of just visiting them in their respective communities. We did not have enough resources for this.

The more than 1,200 responses from the first dialogue phase were included in a qualitative content analysis, which, in comparison with the topics from quality-of-life research, produced twelve topics. Since we had heard many reflections on the question of what makes us special as human beings compared to the computer, the first field was given the title "I: The Individual". Also, we heard fundamental considerations about infrastructure and about the prerequisites that apply to all topics. They were summarized in the second topic "Fundamentals". Without the complete openness regarding content at the beginning of the process, this valuable division would not have been possible. The other topics deal with work & economy, leisure, arts & culture, education, health, environment, traffic & mobility, living together, security, and politics & administration. The first draft visions, indicators, and projects were presented for discussion in a second dialogue phase in 2018/19: Are the descriptions of the desirable futures coherent, or are important aspects missing? Do the proposed indicators make sense and are they already being collected? Do the recommendations for action fit the visions or are important points missing? Are there any other concrete projects that can help us realize the visions?

In the process, the futures literacy of all participants increased, above all through the structured preoccupation with the future. Many assumptions about probable and desirable futures became visible. Also, the future was looked at through two different types of lenses: Digitalization and quality of life. For some actors from the context of digitalization, the focus on quality of life was unusual. Similarly, for some people with a focus on quality of life, the perspective of digitalization was irritating or even unpleasant. At this interface new questions and concrete ideas for action became visible. All vision texts, indicators and action projects, and also four core statements can be found on the process website. The same applies to lists of events and interview partners.

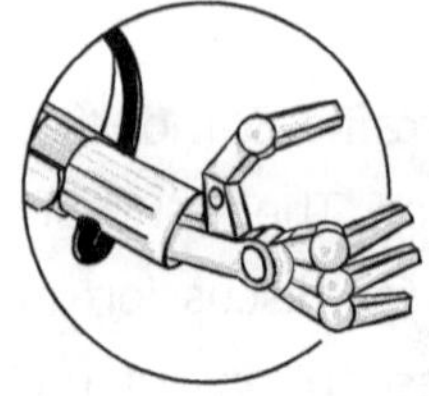

Go ahead

The process #gutlebendigital is just one example of how an important topic can be approached openly in dialogue and without huge resources. There are certainly many important topics.

Which topics are dear to your heart? Can you formulate a good guiding question as described in chapter 2 for one of them? Which groups of participants could you involve with which partners? Then get started. Set up your own dialogue process. Start small. In your organization, your community, or wherever. Not every process needs a societal perspective. Find comrades-in-arms. Do not be discouraged by resistance. Go ahead.

If you would like to have more background information about the #gutlebendigital process, then look at the report on the process at gutlebendigital.de. General questions are addressed in the Quality-of-Life Processes Manual: For example: Do you want to work with or without indicators? How can dialogues be conducted?

Visions
Methods
Innovation
FUTURES
LITERACY

Outlook: Strengthen Futures Literacy

The future is not predetermined. What a relief. What a challenge. To accept the openness of the future as a gift and to deal with it constructively is not easy. But possible. We can strengthen our competency in consciously dealing with open futures, our Futures Literacy. Uncertainty and complexity become less threatening. Our ideas about the future have a great influence on our actions in the present. Our assumptions about the future are very influential - and they can be changed. We can train our imagination, make assumptions visible and experiment with them. Ideally, we do this together with others to harness the collective intelligence of a system and make many different futures visible.

An enhanced Futures Literacy has many advantages. Firstly, a stronger ability to imagine and a greater variety of futures open new options for action today. Futures literacy is a path to more creativity and innovation. It offers room for emergence in complex systems. Secondly, it increases the range of sensors with which we can take in new information. As a result, we can perceive events that we would otherwise not have noticed. New indicators are developed, new ways of obtaining information are explored. The ability to sense and to make sense increases, even for what we can let go. Thirdly, the understanding of today's systems and issues increases when we look at them through the lens of futures. Connections become visible between people and between topics. The same holds for deep-seated causes of current challenges and many activities and projects distributed in the system in the present.

Many methods in the toolbox

This book has shown a variety of ways and methods of using the future today. Starting with dialogue which, in the words of David Bohm (1996), should enable us to consider all views equally so that we can move creatively in a new direction. Dialogue makes the perspectives and assumptions of the various participants visible. At the beginning of a dialogue and any major process on futures there usually is a powerful question that should be relevant to the participants and encourage deeper reflection. Dialogues can be used in small-scale processes without much effort and have the potential to initiate great things. The same applies to appreciative inquiry.

The scenario method presented here offers a more formal approach to the future. Depending on previous experience, the focus on four scenarios can have a massively opening or a restrictive effect. As with each of the methods presented in this book, the aim is to find the appropriate approach to the challenge of the topic, the organization, or the host. Support from experienced process designers is recommended in any case.

With their clear focus and the use of collective intelligence, the methods of visioning and Future Search can make many assumptions and interrelationships visible and unfold great dynamics of action. But they can also have a restrictive effect, as they focus on only one future. One should be aware of this and possibly integrate other methods into a longer process.

Causal Layered Analysis and, above all, Futures Literacy Laboratories offer a particularly high level of innovation. Everything comes together in the Futures Literacy Laboratories: Powerful questions, a high diversity of participants, the dialogue about desirable and probable futures, the (playful) opening to alternative futures, and the orientation towards action.

Also, data and indicators can give the dialogue an additional basis and facilitate the search for priorities for action in the present. Digital tools enable futures processes with many participants and an additional level of cooperation. Playful and artistic approaches, such as card games, sculptures, or improvisation, enable additional enjoyment of futures work, spontaneity, and complementary approaches beyond the analytical.

Act together

The best way to succeed in this futures work is by doing, trying out, and starting together. I hope this book has inspired and encouraged you to do so. No matter in which organization, on which topic, with which networks, with how few resources you are traveling. The examples in the third part are just that: examples that should give you ideas for your specific context. Start small. Experiment with new methods or elements of them. Enjoy working with others. Be open to what you might create. The perfect futures process does not exist. Compromises and even disappointments are inevitable. If your process is better than previous processes, then you have achieved a lot. "Better" may mean that you have included a greater variety of perspectives, or that you have addressed new or better questions, or that you have left more room for emergence. The responsibility does not rest solely on your shoulders. Assume that work on futures issues is also being done in many other places. Feel your way forward, build on what is already there. Do not let book authors tell you what to do or not to do. Enjoy experimenting. Lay the foundation for unforeseeable follow-up projects. For yourself, for your organization, for society. Be the humus on which new activities can grow.

Index